THE LONDONDERRY AIR

JANE ROSS
AND THE FORGOTTEN WITNESS

The Real Origins of Ireland's Most Famous Melody

BRENDAN DRUMMOND

Published in 2014 by Brendan Drummond

ISBN 978-0-9929495-0-1
First Edition
First Impression

Designed by April Sky Design, Newtownards
www.aprilsky.co.uk

Printed by GPS Colour Graphics Ltd, Belfast

A catalogue record for this book is available from the British Library.

CONTENTS

ACKNOWLEDGMENTS

I wish to acknowledge with sincere gratitude the debt I owe to the following for their generous assistance in the completion of this research:

Mr Pete Smith, for putting at my disposal the surviving Ross family papers and letters on the subject of "The Londonderry Air", together with some original musical manuscripts, and family photographs.

My wife, Hazel, for her patient assistance and encouragement at every stage of the research process.

Also her sister, Miss Prunella McCausland, for her skill at deciphering the Rev Manning's handwriting – no easy task at times!

And finally Dr John Moulden, for providing me with a copy of Ms Olivia Maxwell's version of the Manning papers and also some letters from the Sam Henry archive.

The photographs of Jane Ross and Sam Henry may be found on the Northern Ireland Community Archive (www.niarchive.org). The Jane Ross photograph is part of the Sam Henry Collection (Coleraine Museum Service).

The photograph of Denis Hempson is of an engraving from an original drawing by E Scriven.

The Bunting manuscript is reproduced with the kind permission of Queen's University, Belfast.

Pete Smith writes:

When I received an e-mail passing on the address of one Brendan Drummond from an acquaintance, I did not at the time realize the size of the weight which was to be taken from my shoulders.

Brendan explained that he was researching "The Londonderry Air", and asked if I was the grandson of the Rev Manning who was said to be connected to Jane Ross of Limavady, and wondered if I had any papers relating to the subject.

Now, I had been brought up on stories about great aunt Jane and "Name Unknown" as the air was referred to in the family, and had in my possession a plethora of papers including a manuscript book, my grandfather's handwritten account of the discovery of the air and copious notes in his practically illegible handwriting waiting to be worked upon and presented to the world, a task well beyond my capability, but which I somehow felt to be my duty.

A photograph of my grandfather hangs in my saddlery workshop and often when I encounter a problem in my work, I look at the photo, start working on something else and more often than not the solution to my problem occurs to me. Perhaps this was another solved problem.

I don't think Brendan knew the depth of my relief when I gave him these papers to decipher and integrate with his already vast knowledge of the subject. I am convinced that Grandpa would approve of the result.

PREFACE

My interest in "The Londonderry Air" began five years ago when my wife drew my attention to a heated controversy that was then surrounding the origins of the melody, and suggested it should be a subject for some serious research. I was initially dubious. The melody was so famous, so much had been written about it, and the legends surrounding it were so strong – what could I say that had not been said many times before?

My doubts proved unnecessary. I soon realised that while much had indeed been written and spoken about the Air over the past century, most of it, with a few notable exceptions, had been in the form of folklore – based on speculation and long distant memories which were then presented as "facts" with little attention to historical method or musicological practice.

This had, of course, been facilitated by a surprising lack of contemporary written sources. If I was to conduct any form of meaningful research I would, therefore, have to locate some written evidence that had escaped the attention of earlier researchers.

I was fortunate, in this respect, to make the acquaintance of Pete Smith, the closest surviving descendant of the Jane Ross who discovered the melody and the grandson of Canon William Manning, the only member of the Ross family to show a serious interest in its history. Pete kindly put at my disposal all of his grandfather's surviving papers on the subject, along with some interesting musical manuscripts and photographs.

The purpose of this booklet is to give these papers the publicity they deserve and which their writer clearly intended. It will then be up to the reader to decide for themselves the true origins of this most famous of Irish melodies.

Brendan Drummond,
May 2014.

Chapter 1

INTRODUCTION

The melody that is known as "The Londonderry Air", "The Derry Air" or "Danny Boy" has achieved a fame that is unique in the annals of Irish music. For more than a century it has been "world famous" - performed and recorded by countless musicians of every type from opera singers to folk singers, from pop singers to church choirs, from instrumentalists to symphony orchestras. And yet it remains a mystery - a subject of speculation, legends and unending controversy.

The reason is simple - from its sudden appearance in 1855 little has ever been known of its origins - a void that has added to its mystique and fuelled the continuing debate. While the popular mythology that now surrounds it may not be without interest, most of it lacks a basis in fact. More significantly it also ignores the only written account we have of the Air's discovery from a member of the family who were undoubtedly responsible for its preservation.

This account has never before been published. Some of it may not, in fact, have been seen since the day it was written. The purpose of this booklet is to present it in its entirety and allow the reader to make up their own mind as to its veracity.

The account was written by Canon William Robert Fitzgerald Manning, a Church of Ireland rector, and grandnephew of the Miss Jane Ross who first discovered the Air (photo 1). Canon Manning's mother, Sophia Matilda Manning (1857-1914), had been the only daughter of Jane Ross's brother, Canon William Ross, and was thus her only niece (photo 2). She spent much of her youth with her Aunt Jane in Newtownlimavady (or Limavady as it is now known) on the north coast of Ireland, with whom she studied the piano, and "The Londonderry Air" in particular. It was from her Aunt Jane herself that Sophia Matilda learnt the story of the Air's discovery which she passed to her son.

Canon Manning had been aware of the story since 1887 when he was nine, but it was only in 1936, twenty-two years after his mother's sudden death, that he finally decided to commit it to paper. His decision so to do was occasioned by his growing frustration at what he was hearing from "folklore devotees", and the efforts of musicians and poets in their interpretations. He wished to put on record what he knew of the true origin and interpretation of this most famous of Irish melodies. Having completed his account, he left it in his desk to be discovered after his death. He was not a man for publicity.

Canon Manning was born in 1878. He was ordained into the ministry of the Anglican Church of Ireland in 1905. He served as a chaplain at Maryborough (Port Laoise) Prison (1905-1914), and was then Head of the Trinity College Mission in Belfast (1914 - 1917). From 1917 until his death in 1955 he was Rector of the country parish of Kilflynn, Ballyorgan, County Limerick[1], and also Rural Dean.

The Mannings were an interesting family. His grandfather, Robert, had been Chief Engineer of the Board of Works, and had developed a theorem for the drainage of bog land which may still be found in textbooks today. His father, William achieved a less desirable fame, however, when in 1880, as a land agent in Ulster he led a contingent of fifty volunteers from the counties of Cavan and Monaghan to bring in the harvest for a certain Captain Boycott in county Mayo - an infamous event that brought much unhappiness to himself and the family (photo 3).

Canon Manning was a very different person. In his long ministry in Co Limerick he was a friend to all (photos 4, 5 & 6), and won the affection and respect of everyone who knew him, whatever their religious affiliations, as was evident at his funeral.

He was the second of five children. His elder sister, Matilda, died young. His younger sister, Leonore, eloped to South Africa and was never heard of again. His first brother, George, was killed in the Boer war, while his younger brother, Robert, was expelled from school for drinking his headmaster's sherry, and ended up a groom.

He seems to have been a man of many interests and talents. While not a musician himself, due to a deformity in his left hand (suitably concealed in photo 7), he nevertheless developed a considerable skill in the repair and construction of violins, and the story is still told of his sale of an old fiddle to his Bishop on behalf of a poor parishioner. He loved all forms of hunting, was skilled at tying fishing flies, and won shooting trophies at Bisley in spite of having only one hand - a hand which he nearly lost when a bomb exploded in the patrol boat he was using in Belfast docks during the first world war.

His account of the Air's discovery reveals him to have been a man of integrity, and most certainly not a fantasist. He was careful in his choice of words, and not prone to exaggeration. He was simply recording, as accurately as possible, what his mother had told him. Since her words are the only link we have to the world of Jane Ross herself they must be taken seriously. It is to be hoped this booklet will finally give them the publicity they deserve, and their author intended.

The existence of this account had been known for some time, and was occasionally referred to by researchers in the past; but, as far as can be told, only two had actually seen its contents. The first was a Ms Olivia Maxwell, a researcher for a television company, who made a typed copy of much of it in 1981. For some reason, however, the intended programme was never made. And then in 1985 Hugh Shields, of Trinity College Dublin, borrowed and photocopied it - but did not pursue its story. He eventually returned it to its owner, a Mrs A. Smith, after a reminder in 1989, and from that point on it disappeared.

I had been given a copy of Ms Maxwell's typescript by Dr John Moulden, but had little hope of ever uncovering the original. The possibility of locating a "Mrs Smith" or her descendants seemed minimal. In fact, I told my wife I was not even going to try.

Undeterred she set about the task on my behalf, and soon discovered that the authoress Grace Wynne-Jones had moved into Ballyorgan Rectory as a child when her father was appointed Rector after Canon Manning's death. On her website was a message from a Pete Smith who thought he remembered her as a young girl playing in the rectory garden. Could this Pete Smith be related to the Mrs A. Smith?

I contacted Grace Wynne-Jones with my problem, and she kindly enquired of Pete if he would welcome an approach from a researcher who might be interested in his family's history. His response was encouraging. His grandfather had indeed been the Canon William Manning I was seeking, and he had spent many happy holidays with him in his rectory in Co Limerick (photo 8). It then transpired we had attended the same school in Belfast.

I was particularly excited to hear that Pete still possessed his grandfather's papers on the subject of "The Londonderry Air", including the account of which I had a copy. He also had the handwritten music book of Miss Theodosia Ross, Jane's younger sister and helper in her folk song research, and another manuscript which he said was in the handwriting of Canon Manning's mother, Sophia Matilda Manning, who had, of course, studied the Air with Jane herself. Both manuscripts contained a copy of "The Londonderry Air", which made them the only surviving versions of the melody from members of the Ross family.

A few minor problems remained, however - Pete was resident in Germany, where he had lived for most of his working life - and he had to find where he had put the papers. Neither problem proved insurmountable, however. As Pete and his wife, Dagmar, had planned a holiday in Ballyorgan we arranged to meet there (photo 9), where he presented me with the complete Ross archive and insisted I retain it for two years, when he hoped to return for another holiday. I was overwhelmed by his generosity, and conscious of the responsibility I had now assumed for its safety. This was an offer of which all previous researchers could only have dreamt.

The significance of the archive was soon apparent. With Pete's permission it would have to be published and Canon Manning's words given the publicity they clearly merited, but had been denied for so long. To be fully appreciated, however, they needed to be presented in their historical and musical contexts. It was necessary, therefore, to begin with as accurate an account as possible of the Air's known history.

It was soon apparent that this would only be achieved by focusing on the written sources. The oral traditions, however strong, would have to be discounted. Not only were they of comparatively recent appearance, they were also contradictory, and in some cases fanciful in the extreme.

The picture that emerged of the Air's origins and development is surprisingly coherent, if very different from the versions that are usually recounted.

Chapter 2

THE HISTORY OF THE AIR

The story of the "The Londonderry Air" begins in the year 1855 when the melody first appeared in a volume entitled "The Ancient Music of Ireland"[2]. All we know of its origins is what we are told by the editor, George Petrie, in his introduction:

Name unknown.

For the following beautiful air I have to express my grateful acknowledgement to Miss J. Ross, of N.-T.-Limavady, in the county of Londonderry - a lady who has made a large collection of the popular unpublished melodies of that county, which she has very kindly placed at my disposal, and which has added very considerably to the stock of tunes which I had previously acquired from that still very Irish county. I say still very Irish; for though it has been planted for more than two centuries by English and Scottish settlers, the old Irish race still forms the great majority of its peasant inhabitants; and there are few, if any, counties in which, with less foreign admixture, the ancient melodies of the country have been so extensively preserved. The name of the tune unfortunately was not ascertained by Miss Ross, who sent it to me with the simple remark that it was "very old," in the correctness of which statement I have no hesitation in expressing my perfect concurrence.

Petrie's words reveal little of the melody's origins - he merely states he had received it from a Miss Jane Ross of Limavady, who said it was "very old". And that is all we know. It should be stressed that Jane Ross never revealed where she heard the melody, when she heard the melody, who played it to her, or what it was called. Any claims that she did are pure fiction. So too is the common assertion that it was Petrie who gave it the title "The Londonderry Air". His title was the much more mundane - "Name unknown".

Who then were George Petrie and Jane Ross?

George Petrie (1789-1866) was a Dubliner of Scottish ancestry. He was a man of many talents - a gifted painter, an antiquarian, an archaeologist, and an amateur violinist with a keen interest in Irish folk music, of which he was one of the leading collectors of his day. He had been an admirer of the earlier collector, Edward Bunting (1773-1843), to whom he donated a number of melodies, eleven of which were published by Bunting as piano solos in his volume of 1840[3]. However, he was also critical of Bunting's collecting methods, stating in his introduction to "The Ancient Music of Ireland" that the harpers and other instrumentalists who were Bunting's main sources were "usually the least to be trusted" because of the "absurd indulgence of barbarous licenses and conventionalities" with which they interpreted the melodies (p.xvi) - a statement of considerable relevance to any consideration of "The Londonderry Air". In Petrie's opinion singers were the only reliable source of genuine Irish melody.

In addition to his other interests Petrie also helped compile the "Ordnance Survey Memoirs" for the Roe Valley (1833-1835) which encompassed Limavady, and was thus well aware of the music of the area[4].

Jane Ross (1810-1879) is a much more elusive figure (photo 10). A mural of her in the Main Street of Limavady illustrates the public perception, with its casual appearance and references to "Danny Boy" (photo 11). The reality was very different. Jane was a member of the gentry. Her family could trace its roots to a "John Rosse" who had been one of the original twelve burgesses of the town appointed by King James 1st. Her father, John Ross (1778-1830), had commanded the Limavady Yeomanry, and on the passing of the Act of Union between Ireland and England in 1800 had been given all the muniments, seal and corporation records of the dissolved borough for safe keeping. He had first married an Elizabeth McCausland of Fruit Hill (now Drenagh), but this marriage was childless. His second marriage (1809) was to his cousin Jane Ogilby (1778-1858) of Ardnargle House. Both the McCausland and Ogilby families were prominent landowners in the area. This second marriage resulted in six children:

Jane	(1810-1879)
Elizabeth	(1812-1889)
William	(1814-1891)
Anne	(1817-1864)
Theodosia	(1819-1875)
John	(1821-1878)

Jane spent her first thirteen years at the Lodge, a large house with extensive grounds at the end of the Main Street in Limavady (photo 12). In 1823 her father sold this house and its demesne for £6,001-2-9, a considerable sum in those days[5]. The following year a "John Ross, Magistrate," is mentioned as living in the Main Street[6]. What appears to be his widow and family are then recorded in the 1831 census as living with four servants in no. 68 Main street[7], though the actual street numbers are unlikely to be the same as today. In 1846 a "Mrs Jane Ross" is listed under "gentry" as still living in the Main Street[8]. The first mention of the "Misses Ross" as living in the Main Street comes in September 1855 when both they and a Mrs Ross are listed as having responded to a call for "illuminations" to celebrate the capture of Sebastopol[5]. In the Griffith's Valuation of 1858, however, the only "Rosses" in the Main Street were a "Mary Ross" and an "Amelia Ross", though a "Jane Ross" was included as the lessor of a number of properties in the adjoining Market Street and Irish Green[9]. By 1870 "The Misses Ross" were certainly living in no. 51 Main Street[10] – in the house that is now associated with them, where Jane remained until her death (photo 13).

None of the sisters married, but Jane's lifelong interest in traditional music was shared by her sister Theodosia and brother William. Their graves are recorded on a memorial stone in the graveyard of Christ Church Limavady, the Anglican church where the family had worshipped for many generations (photos 14 & 15).

The early history of "The Londonderry Air" may be summarised as follows:

In 1855 the melody first appeared in George Petrie's "The Ancient Music of Ireland".

In 1879 Jane Ross died at the age of sixty-nine without having revealed its origins, and unaware of the fame it would soon attain.

In 1882 the Air appeared in the "Songs of Old Ireland" in an arrangement by Stanford to the words "Emer's Farewell to Culcullain"[11].

In 1894 the description (but not the title) "Londonderry Air" was first given to the melody when it was included in the "Irish Song Book" to the words: "Would God I were the tender apple blossom", and entitled "Irish Love Song"[12].

In 1902 the Air was introduced to a wider audience when the Australian composer Percy Grainger (1882-1961), then resident in London, made the first of his settings of the melody.

In 1913 Grainger made the first recording of the melody.

Also in 1913 the words "Danny Boy" were published as an accompaniment to the melody. They had already been written in 1910 by Fred Weatherly (1848-1929), an English lawyer and songwriter. Weatherly had never in fact visited Ireland, let alone Limavady, but when his sister-in-law from Colorado introduced him to "The Londonderry Air" in 1912 he was able to adapt his words to the new melody with little alteration[13]. They did not meet with universal approval, however. A. P. Graves, who had written the earlier texts for the melody was particularly irritated by their "plaintive" style, which may well have been inspired by the unfortunate fact that the year 1910 had seen the deaths of Weatherly's father and his only son[14]. Whatever one's opinion of the "Danny Boy" words, it must be conceded they do convey the spirit of the melody with greater success than any other setting, before or since, and have added immeasurably to the Air's ultimate fame. It should be noted in passing that the often repeated claim that Weatherly's sister-in-law had heard the melody being sung by gold prospectors from the Limavady area[27] has no basis in fact. Her husband had emigrated to Colorado in the hope of making his fortune in silver mining[13].

In 1915 the melody was recorded to the "Danny Boy" words by the internationally renowned opera singer, Ernestine Schumann-Heink. This recording was highly successful and signals the start of the Air's world-wide fame - a fame that was quickly enhanced by the newly emerging broadcasting stations, and the ready availability of cheap sheet music.

It is interesting to reflect that Jane Ross never knew the titles "The Londonderry Air" or "Danny Boy", and that whoever "Danny Boy" might be, he originally had no relationship whatsoever with Ireland.

As the fame of the Air increased, so too did the interest in its origins. An article in the "Musical Times" of August 1918 by Henry Coleman (the organist of St Columb's Church of Ireland cathedral in Derry) claimed it had belonged as much to County Donegal as County Londonderry[15], while similar claims were made for County Cork in August 1924, in a letter to the press from W. H. Grattan Flood (a copy of which may be found in the Manning papers). Speculation was rife, and the legends were taking shape. What were the true origins of the melody? Who was Jane Ross? And where had she really discovered it?

Matters came to a head in August 1928 with the publication of a number of letters in the press in England and Ireland. These began in the "Sunday Times" of the 5th of August with a query from a Mrs S. Norman as to the origins of the Air, noting it had been performed at the funeral of the actress Ellen Terry. This elicited many replies over the following weeks. In the first Fred Weatherly explained his "Danny Boy" words, and quoted "his friend" A. P. Graves as saying it was collected by a "Miss Anna Ross" and published by Petrie in 1857 (sic). Henry Coleman also wrote to draw attention to his article of 1918. The most significant response to Mrs Norman's letter, however, came from a Major John Riky:

Sir,
"The Londonderry Air" was rescued from oblivion by the late Miss Galway (sic) (about fifty years ago). She heard it played by an itinerant musician on the street in Limavady, Co. Londonderry. Miss Galway (sic), an old lady, herself well skilled in music, jotted down, with much care, the tune, and brought it to her friend the Rev. Canon Armstrong (the celebrated musician, organist and composer) to whom she entrusted her MSS. Canon Armstrong harmonised the tune and became the first musician to do so.

John Riky (Major) L. R. A. M., (Dublin).
Clapham Common SW

This letter appeared to be riddled with inaccuracies. The Air had, of course, been "rescued from oblivion" by Miss Jane Ross, at least twenty-five years earlier than 1878, and the Rev James Armstrong (1840-1928), while later the rector and organist of Castlerock Parish Church in Co Londonderry, would have been little more than ten years old at the time of the Air's discovery. Who then were this Major Riky and Miss Galway?

Major Riky was not easy to identify. However, an on-line search of contemporary military records revealed one person only of that name and rank[16]. This John Riky was born in 1858, the second son of the Rev Walter Riky, rector of Ballyshannon, Co Donegal, on the north-western coast of Ireland. In the earlier part of his military career he was a Captain in the 5th battalion of the Inniskilling Fusiliers[17] (who interestingly adopted "The Londonderry Air" as their Funeral March, having been introduced to it in 1915, according to a letter in the "Belfast Telegraph" of 17th September 1963). He is later listed as a Major in the Northumberland Fusiliers[18]. This Major Riky resided in Mount Hall, Killygordon, County Donegal, where he became a magistrate for the county, and was on the roll for High Sheriff in 1903. He is recorded as having collected one Irish melody himself, a version of "The Hawk of Ballyshannon"[19]. His death is listed in Windsor in 1930, aged 72. The details of his life are, therefore, entirely consistent with him having been the writer of the letter. As a magistrate he was presumably a reliable witness. How then did he get his facts so wrong?

Miss Honoria Tomkins Galwey (1830-1925) was also a child of the rectory. Her father, the Venerable Charles Galwey had been rector of Moville in Co Donegal from 1830 to 1852, and Archdeacon of Derry from 1860 to 1873. It is quite possible, therefore, that the Major and Miss Galwey were known to each other. Be that as it may, Honoria had a lifelong interest in Irish music and collected many traditional melodies which she published in 1910 in a volume entitled "Old Irish Croonauns"[20]. Number 4 among these, "Pigeon in the Gate", was, she says, noted on the street in Moville in 1849 from the playing of a blind fiddler known as "Paddy the Slithers", and harmonised by Canon Armstrong - but is not in any way similar to "The Londonderry Air". Could this nevertheless be the source of the Major's letter, and the legend of the Limavady street musician? While it was Miss Galwey who had told Henry Coleman "The Londonderry Air" belonged "as much to County Donegal as County Derry"[15] she never claimed for herself the honour of having "rescued it from oblivion", in spite of living to ninety-four years of age and witnessing its growing fame. Henry Coleman, who could remember Miss Galwey as an old lady in Derry cathedral, provides an interesting detail to her life in a letter to the "Belfast Newsletter" of the 28th September 1963 when he states she had been a "friend" of Jane Ross, but one can only speculate on the relevance, if any, of this remark.

It is just possible, however, that the Major's letter may not be as totally inaccurate as it first seemed. Some of his claims may, indeed, have a basis in history. He might even be describing an actual event that happened around 1878 on the Main Street in Limavady. His basic premise, however, that "The Londonderry Air" was first noted at that time by Honoria Galwey is clearly inaccurate. Apart from the factual errors in this claim, she would not have been "an old lady" at the time.

In spite of this, his letter did have a number of consequences:

Firstly, it elicited the earliest written statement from a member of the Ross family on the subject of the Air. In a letter to the "Sunday Times" of the 19th August 1928 the Rev J. T. Trelawny-Ross D. D., the eldest son of Jane's brother William, wrote from his home in Ham House, Plymouth to correct the Major's errors, and the statement by A. P. Graves that the Air had first been collected by a "Miss Anna Ross". It had been his aunt, Miss Jane Ross, whose "delightful piano playing" he could well remember, who had found and preserved the Air for publication in 1855. He sent a similar missive to the "Northern Whig" which was printed on the 21st August. (This is reproduced in full in chapter 8).

Secondly, it attracted the attention of researchers to Ham House and the Trelawny-Rosses. But as we shall see, that side of the family never knew much about the Air, and nothing of interest has ever been uncovered there in spite of many searches. As Brian Audley was to discover in 1994 the only material relating to the Air to be found there consisted of modern newspaper cuttings[21].

Thirdly, and most significantly, it inspired the legend that the Air was first written down by Jane Ross from the playing of a traditional fiddler on the Main Street in Limavady. The fact that no record of this event could be found in the seventy-five years before the Major's letter has in no way dampened the enthusiasm of its proponents. While the legend cannot be wholly discounted, it should always be remembered that it was a Miss Honoria Galwey who was first associated with the alleged event, and that the legend itself was unknown to the Ross family at the time, as will become apparent.

In spite of such obvious problems, the legend of the street musician quickly gained momentum, due in no small part to the writings and broadcasts of a local journalist, Sam Henry (1878-1952). Henry was a man of many talents, with a keen interest in local folklore, folk music, poetry, genealogy, photography, bird watching and archaeology. When he gave a talk he could also entertain his audiences on the fiddle and the tin whistle (photo 16). From 1923 to 1939 he edited the weekly series, "Songs of the People" in the Northern Constitution newspaper. His interest in "The Londonderry Air" dates at least from December 1923 when he commented on it in his column and asked his readers if they knew of any old words or titles for the melody[21].

In 1934 Henry received a letter from a Frank Thomson in Canada who stated he had bought a fiddle around 1911-1912 in Ballymena, County Antrim, from a street musician named McCormick, who told him the instrument had belonged to his father who had used it to play "The Londonderry Air" to someone called Ross in Limavady. Even though some eighty-one years had by then elapsed since the alleged event, Henry took this claim very seriously. He did not consider the obvious possibility that the story was a form of sales talk, or find it surprising that anyone would wish to sell a fiddle with such a famous provenance.

Henry was further impressed by Thomson's suggestion that the melody had been entitled "Rory's Lament" or "O'Cahan's Tune". Writing in 1939 to the Rev W. T. Trelawny-Ross, who had by then inherited Ham House from his father, the Rev J. T. Trelawny-Ross, he summarises the results of his research:

"The strong local tradition is that a fiddler named John McCormick played the tune in the street opposite the Alexander Arms, Limavady. Miss Jane Ross --- heard the tune, took the fiddler in, gave him hospitality, and learnt it. --- I am convinced it was composed by Rory Dall O'Cahan --- . Its theme is the glory and the eclipse of the O'Cahan Clan at the Plantation of Ulster --- ". (More of this letter is reproduced in chapter 8).

It should be pointed out that the "strong local tradition" that the melody was first noted on the Main Street in Limavady had been unknown to Henry in the first eleven years of his research. It seems to date from the Thomson letter!

The suggestion that the Air had been composed by Rory Dall O'Cahan was not new. It dated from an article by Mrs Milligan Fox in 1912[22]. As Brian Audley has demonstrated, however, her linking of the Air with the harper O'Cahan was not only misleading but inaccurate[21], and based on speculation alone. The speculative nature of her claim was confirmed by Mrs Fox's sister, Alice, in a letter to the "Northern Whig" of the 22nd August 1928, and also by a local writer on musical affairs, Samuel Leighton, in a letter to the same newspaper on the 30th of that month. In spite of this, the melody has continued to be attributed to the harper O'Cahan in some quarters, and has even been given the title "O'Cahan's Lament"[23].

The blind harper and composer, Rory Dall O'Cahan (c1570-1650), was a near relation of Sir Donnell O'Cahan, the Chieftain of the clan. He spent most of his life after 1601 in Scotland where he eventually died. His only recorded "Lament" is "Rory Dall's Sister's Lament"[24], a Scottish tune in no way related to the "The Londonderry Air".

The Rev W. T. Trelawny-Ross was not entirely impressed by this letter from Sam Henry, commenting to his cousin, Canon William Manning: "I wonder if he is to be relied on" (see chapter 8). In spite of his doubts, however, the legend of the street musician has persisted to the present day.

In 1979 it was given fresh impetus when precisely the same claims emerged for another fiddler named McCurry (1830-1910)[25]. By then some 126 years had elapsed since the alleged event, but this in no way lessened the zeal of his supporters[26]. The "strong local tradition" in support of McCormick was now replaced by "strong oral evidence" in support of McCurry. As before, the actual strength of the "evidence" was neither specified nor evaluated. The fact that it was unknown to Brian Audley and Hugh Shields, both of whom had spent some thirty years researching the music of the area was conveniently overlooked. The story was further elaborated by the claim that the fairies may have played the melody to Rory Dall O'Cahan, by now a "Chieftain of the Clan", when he was inebriated. When he was sober he then "entertained the guests with the first rendition of the air that was to be taken down by Jane Ross some 250 years later"![27] We have entered the world of fantasy!

The claims for both fiddlers pose the same problems for their adherents in that neither claim has any basis in fact other than some very distant family memories. Neither fiddler could have been more than twenty years old at the time concerned, and both belonged to the Scots-Irish tradition rather than the Gaelic from which the melody most certainly emerged. Petrie's words in his introduction to the Air that "there are few, if any, counties in which, with less foreign admixture, the ancient melodies of the country have been so extensively preserved" is of particular relevance here.

The main reason for questioning such claims, however, is that they are flatly contradicted by Canon William Manning's account of 1936, as will soon become apparent.

Chapter 3

THE MUSIC OF THE AIR

The musical quality of “The Londonderry Air” has never been in doubt. As early as 1893 Hubert Parry, when discussing Irish folk tunes in general, could describe it as “one of the most perfect in existence”[28]. While few will question this judgement, it marks the limit of any consensus. The musical nature of the melody has proved as contentious as its origins:

Is it	(a)	a genuine Irish folk song?
	(b)	an adaptation of an Irish folk song?
	(c)	an original composition?

Each of these theories has had its proponents. Havergal Brian, the English composer and critic, first heard the Air in 1904 or 1905, in a performance by the Halle orchestra of Stanford’s “Irish Rhapsody”. After some thirty years of reflection he came to the conclusion that the melody was “of no great age”, and that it had been composed by Miss Jane Ross herself, “and that shyness alone robbed her of the fame”[29]. This was, and remains an idiosyncratic suggestion.

Anne Gilchrist’s article of 1934 “A New Light Upon The Londonderry Air” is more closely reasoned. As an expert in folk music she was puzzled by the Air’s sudden appearance “full-grown, without ancestry, collaterals, or descendants, in the form of the variants one would have expected to find in the case of any current folk-air”[30]. Moreover, it did not fit any recognised Irish metre, and no words were known to have accompanied it. Taking the advice of the Irish scholar, D J O’Sullivan, that the printed version falsified its rhythm and metre but would fit a well known Irish stanza called “Ochtfochlech bec”, she concluded that its quadruple rhythm was incorrect, and should have been triple. She speculated that Jane Ross had been deceived by the rubato with which it was originally played to her.

This theory must be taken seriously. As we have seen, Petrie himself had criticised the “barbarous licences” which instrumentalists took with their melodies, and Manning’s account will relate how Jane was never satisfied with his printed version of her Air. Gilchrist’s suggested triple time version is musically convincing and in the known style of a genuine Irish ballad-air.

Hugh Shields, an acknowledged expert in the folk music of the Limavady area, was impressed by her "intelligent article". In his "New Dates for Old Songs"[31] of 1979 he casts further doubts on the authenticity of the Air, noting that its "melodic compass is greater, and the phrases longer, than those of any known traditional Irish vocal air". He also pointed out its similarity to an earlier song air "Aislean an Oigfear" or "The Young Man's Dream", which was, as Gilchrist suggested, in triple time. This had been copied by Edward Bunting in 1796 on his visit to the home of the harper, Denis Hempson (c1695-1807) (photo 17). Hempson (or O'Hampsey, to give him the Irish version of his name) lived in Magilligan, some ten miles from Limavady. He was the last of the great Irish harpers and represented a tradition that was no longer in fashion. Bunting's manuscript[32] reveals the difficulties he experienced in attempting to notate the playing of the elderly harper in the days before tape recording (photo 18). He could not decipher the higher passage at the end, and simply gave up. His published version omits it entirely[33] (photo 19). In spite of this omission, Shields linking of "The Young Man's Dream" with "The Londonderry Air" is now widely accepted. The development of the familiar final section of the Air was, in Shields' words, the result of "the keyboard divagations of a middle class lady who like her sister played the piano and lived in a small country town, not ten miles from Hempson's former dwelling".

Gilchrist and Shields agree, therefore, that the Air as we now have it is an adaptation of an older Irish melody, rather than an accurate transcription of the original music. This seems a reasonable theory. When one recalls the difficulty experienced by Bunting, the professional musician, in his transcription, how much more demanding must it have been for an amateur like Jane Ross to copy down?

With their expertise in folk music one might have expected the verdict of Gilchrist and Shields to have been definitive. Not so. In his "The Provenance of the Londonderry Air"[34] of 2000 Brian Audley argues that it developed naturally from "The Young Mans' Dream" and other melodies through "the process of tradition" - its repetition and variation by different performers in different places and times.

Audley's survey of the Air's history is authoritative and dispassionate, and a welcome corrective to most writing on the subject. His musicological methodology is less convincing, however. Quoting Honoria Galwey's statement that the Air had been sung in County Donegal to the words "Oh Shrive Me, Father"[15] he traces the source of these words to an 1814 volume by Fitzsimons, E & Smith, J: "Irish Minstrelsy: A Selection of the Original

Melodies of Ireland with Characteristic Words by Edward Fitzsimons, Esq. and Symphonies and Accompaniments by Mr. J. Smith"[35]. He claims their presence in this volume proves Anne Gilchrist was "wrong" in her statement "The Londonderry Air" had lacked a text before its appearance in 1855. However, the tune to which it is set in this 1814 volume is not "The Londonderry Air" but a version of "Castle Hyde" which has little obvious relationship to the Air itself. The fact that these non-traditional English words would have fitted "The Londonderry Air", as we now know it, does not prove they were ever sung to it by the native Irish prior to Petrie's publication in 1855. The reality is that native singers were highly unlikely to have encountered such a volume in their daily lives and could never have afforded its purchase price if they had. And they would not have been interested in it anyway, due to its classical content and their lack of literacy – musical and otherwise.

Here and elsewhere the visual links between melodies which Audley claims to find on paper are not apparent to the ear, as one would surely have expected in music of the folk tradition.

The "Ordnance Survey Memoirs of Ireland"(vol.15)[36] are of interest here. They encompass the Dungiven area, south of Limavady, where the old Gaelic culture remained strong and distinct, and where, as will be seen, Jane Ross probably encountered her famous Air. These "Memoirs" include (pages 37 & 38) a catalogue of local songs collected by a James McCloskey. There is no mention in it of "Oh Shrive Me, Father", but there is included a melody called "The Groves of Blarney" - an acknowledged variant of "The Young Man's Dream". The melody which Bunting copied down in 1796 was, therefore, still being performed in the Dungiven area some thirty-five years later, but not to Audley's proposed text. It is simply not credible to believe it could have "naturally" mutated into "The Londonderry Air" within a further twenty years, for Jane Ross to copy it down.

The origins and musical nature of the Air remain as controversial today as they were in 1936 when Canon Manning finally decided to put pen to paper. Had his words been available then, the current debates would probably have been unnecessary. It is time to let these words speak for themselves.

Chapter 4

THE MANNING PAPERS

Manning's account of the Air's discovery is contained in several exercise books. It will be presented in three chapters. Further chapters will include his notes and reflections, and the correspondence he entered into with relatives and researchers.

His handwriting throughout is a problem, being difficult to decipher at the best of times and particularly so when he is making changes. Any doubtful words will be represented by (?), and indecipherable phrases by --- (?).

He begins by explaining why it has taken him so long to put pen to paper.

In the preface to his valuable work on Ancient Irish Music published in London in 1796, Edward Bunting wrote: "It is a debt which every man owes to his country, to search for and perpetuate the records of other days, to oppose as far as he can, the destructive ravages of time, and to render permanent the fleeting productions of every species of genius".

Reading these words in a cursory glance at Bunting's edition a friend permitted me some fifteen or sixteen years ago, intensified the "urge" which I had experienced for many years previously in a less degree that I set down in writing what I knew of the origin and especially of the interpretation of the "Londonderry Air" (so called!). But fully aware that the mere "narrative necessities" of such a history and interpretation, and in order to "get it over" as helpfully as possible to the really interested, entailed publication of personal and family matters, otherwise out of place, involved considerations of personal literary qualifications, also the dangers of misunderstanding and unsympathetic criticism, I was naturally reluctant to embark upon such an uncertain sea.

However, coupled with that long present "urge" several causes have combined of late to conquer all deterring influences; amongst these I may mention three as outstanding:

(1) The efforts of otherwise well informed and erudite folklore devotees who appear to me at least to approach this air with preconceived opinions regarding its interpretation and try to reduce it to the limits of a formula or make it conform to the set rules and standards they have found applicable elsewhere. But, I ask, is it ever really possible scientifically or satisfactorily to account

for any of the "fleeting productions of Genius"? The same question in another context seems to have impressed J. McDonnell when he wrote to Bunting "Be sure to explain" etc.

(2) As far as I am aware, up to the present (1936) there are twenty-one published settings to this air by artists who have made their mark in the musical world but were unacquainted with the circumstances and spirit underlying its composition. None of these agree with the interpretation I heard over fifty years ago from one I believe well calculated to give a true rendering of the air as conceived by its composer, or at least as close as possible to the impression he intended to convey to his early hearers, and through them bequeath to posterity. In addition to the efforts of the composers and instrumentalists there are the well intentioned efforts of the poets and propagandists, great and small, to put words to this tune as they know it, but for reasons set forth later on I must consider all attempts as not only misguided but entirely out of place.

(3) Last but not least, I am constantly listening to many and various and unsatisfying renderings of this "air" on the air particularly from the Irish Free State Broadcasting Station. Coupled with this a Director of that Broadcasting Station was reported in the public press to have mildly censured a certain element who would wish to have "the Londonderry Air ad nauseam"!! All of which is disquieting, not to say hurtful, to the feelings of one who was brought up to love that air, to respect the spirit of its composer and the circumstances under which it came to him.

For above reasons, sharpened by a sense of duty and a tinge of self reproach, brushing aside all personal considerations I must now commit myself and my story to the dangers of misunderstanding, to literary and musical criticism, and set down as simply, intelligibly and briefly as I can what I know of this so called "Londonderry Air".

I shall be satisfied if only my poor efforts may promote a better understanding of its message and may perhaps in some small way hand on something of that strange sense of awe and reverence with which I first listened to it and had unfolded to me the moving story of its coming from those regions we know of but can so little define or locate.

Manning wrote these words in 1936, twenty-two years after the sudden death of his mother who had been, of course, the source of his information. It seems he had intended to put pen to paper for some time, but had been reluctant so to do because of family considerations and a lack of confidence

in his own ability. It is interesting to note the factors that finally overcame this reluctance:
(i) the misguided approach of "folklore devotees"
(ii) the misguided interpretations of musicians and poets
(iii) the unceasing publicity given to incorrect "renderings of the Air" by broadcasters.

Manning's initial quotation from Bunting appears to come from the preface to Bunting's second volume which was published in London in 1809[37], but was sometimes described as his first. The original words were:

"It is a debt which we owe to our country and to truth, to search the record of other days, and to oppose the ravages of time." Manning's slight inaccuracies here are understandable in that he had only been given a "cursory glance" at the edition some fifteen or sixteen years earlier. J. McDonnell was a Doctor James McDonnell, an amateur harpist, who had helped to organise the Belfast Harpers' Festival of 1792[38]. The quotation beginning: "Be sure to explain" is contained in a letter from Dr McDonnell to Bunting which is reproduced in the "Annals of the Irish Harpers" (page 279)[39].

Manning continues with some family history:

The History of the Londonderry air (so called).

Somewhere towards the end of the sixteenth century there arrived in the North of Ireland from Scotland a member of a titled family (title now extinct) named John Ross - sometimes spelt Rosse in the old manuscripts. This man eventually settled down and acquired considerable property at Limavady in the County Londonderry. He was one of the twelve Burgesses to whom, with a Provost, King James the 1st of England granted the Charter of Limavady in the year 1612. According to old family traditions - oral and written - he brought with him from Scotland considerable property of a portable kind including jewellery etc. One item of the latter is before me as I write. It is a ladies ring made of fine gold beautifully designed and chased even in the parts invisible when the ring is on the finger. My mother refers to it in her brief account of her jewellery compiled in 1904 in the following terms: "The old ring with brownish stone - Topaz - in centre and two small diamonds at each side set in silver is very old. Aunt Jane Ross used to wear it. Father had evidence it was brought from Scotland by the Ross who first came to Ireland". She told me it was greatly prized in the family by its various possessors as an heirloom and by none more than by her Aunt Jane Ross who frequently wore it. She treated it with an unusual care and reverence principally on account of its history and associations which appealed to an element in her nature she was always ready, as we shall see later on, to respond to, and which apparently developed into an obsession in her declining years. Mother, in her young days, was in constant intercourse with this Aunt Jane and even resided with her for a while and apparently long enough for her aunt to discover that by nature she was like-minded with herself and the most likely of her younger generation growing up around her to give the ring the homage due to it. Accordingly she gave Mother the ring, and she with the same end in view gave it to me as I have now given it to my daughter. Apparently John Ross brought over with him something of more permanent value than money and jewels in that he brought with him and transmitted to his descendants that strong undefinable Scottish homing instinct and reverence for the dignified old which is such a marked feature of many of the writings of Sir W. Scott and Robbie Burns, stands out prominently in R. L. S. and frequently peeps out unexpectedly in other writers. I merely mention this incident of the ring and its associations as a helpful stepping stone into that little side world which was once the parish of the few but now promises to become the province of the many through the efforts, laudable and otherwise, of the various folk-lore societies. Sometimes the subconscious mind, unbidden and for no apparent reason at the moment, becomes very active and asserts itself sufficiently to obtrude its movements on our attention so that incidents, sometimes the most trivial, of our childhood are clearer and more real to us than those of a week ago. When such occasions occur it is not a bad plan, if the memories are of any pleasure or value to others or even oneself, to take a pen at once and note down the fleeting though very real pictures of the past. A further and very leisurely exercise of no mean value will be the verifying and noting of the historical accuracy, coordination and resultant value of these random memories.

I have pursued this idea or ideal - call it what you will - for the past few years and from the sheaf of notes so garnered I cull the following concerning the "Air" under consideration.

It should be noted from the above that Manning's mother was "in constant intercourse with this Aunt Jane and even resided with her for a while". Her words must be taken seriously.

He now describes his own first encounter with the Air, at the age of eight:

On a dry, cold, but very sunny morning in October 1886 there arrived unexpectedly at our temporary house 10 miles from Railway (?) station in the County Kildare a white haired dapper little man carrying a black brief bag.

With (?) tall hat and gloves and all he might have passed for a member of the legal Profession or a Doctor on his morning rounds. As a matter of fact he was an itinerant piano tuner, a general favourite, whom we all called, affectionately if somewhat familiarly, "Old Moffatt".

He had come some distance on foot and mother insisted on his having something approaching a second breakfast. This over he went to tune the piano in the drawing room. This room faced south and a high window admitted the full glare of the sun to the fire at which I sat watching its dancing flames vying with the sun playing on them. There I sat waiting rather impatiently for "Old Moffatt" to finish tuning that piano of lovely tone - an Erard if I remember rightly. Every moment seemed an hour to me as I wanted him to play a violin that my mother, yielding to my importunity - had bought for me though she must have known at the time that I could never play it satisfactorily to myself or anyone else owing to the loss of my left hand. Presently the tuning was complete to the old man's satisfaction and he asked me to call mother. She came at once and sitting down tried over the octaves etc and glided with seeming unconsciousness into the air under consideration which she played over three times each different, rendering it according to her accustomed manner. Impatient though I was for the violin's turn to come along I could not help noticing the remarkable effect on the old tuner as he sat listening with strained attention. The "Air" ended he hurriedly rose to his feet with unconcealed excitement, his eyes glistening as he blurted out "What's its name, are there any words to it?"

Turning around on the piano stool to face him mother replied quietly "It has no name and there are no words to it - there never could be"!! He regarded her for a few seconds in silence - turned and gazed out of the window with a faraway look in his eyes, turned back and replied in a hushed almost awe stricken tone of voice with "Yes, I can see that"!!

Again he lapsed into a preoccupied mood but I soon recalled him to (?) and the violin. Taking it up he turned it and, while playing it firmly but gently, pointed out to me the impossibility of my ever being able to play this instrument I had set my heart on. I must have shown my disappointment for the kindly old soul added quietly: "But perhaps some day when you grow up you will make one"! Firmly with all the vim I could muster at the moment, I answered him "I will", and I have kept my promise so far that I have made several, and repaired and restored hundreds experiencing indescribable pleasure in doing so.

(Looking back now over the intervening half century I often wonder did this dear old man realise at that moment that he was actually giving me a practical rendering and application to life of that air itself to which he had just been

listening. I believe he did and so I conclude this second incident in my story and say to him "Thank you old Moffatt. Your kindly encouragement still lives with me, just as it still lives in that air (?) in spite of its repeated mutilation".)

The summer succeeding the above incident was remarkable for its astounding heat and drought rendering the parched fields exceptionally hard as I found to my cost when I had a fall out riding on the flat and broke a collar bone. During recovery I had to keep quiet and frequently lay on a rug spread on a grass plot beside the house where mother would come as often as she could to keep me company. On one of these occasions she brought a book of Tennyson's poems and some lines she read out about words connecting the soul within started in my mind a train of thought leading back to the incident at the piano tuning. I questioned her about the origin and meaning of that air I had heard her play so often and always in the same manner. In response she told me or rather seemed to rehearse it in almost measured mode the following story which I gathered she got from Aunt Jane and which I repeat as nearly as I can remember.

This passage gives an interesting description of Manning's early life towards the end of the nineteenth century. It also introduces us to his deformed left hand and his determination to make and repair violins, even if he could never play them. In later years he attempted to discover more about "Old Moffatt", but without success - like most tuners he was probably self-employed. The real significance of the passage, however, lies in its description of his mother's interpretation of the Air, which she played through three times "each different, rendering it according to her accustomed manner", which contrasts with the "repeated mutilation" to which it was later subjected. "It had no name and there are no words to it - there never could be".

His mother's hand written version of the Air (photo 20), which presumably reflects what she had learnt from Jane Ross herself, is of considerable interest here – the repeat marks at the end (unique to this version) indicating the melody was to be played more than once, as just described.

Manning then records his mother's account of the Air's discovery, as received from her Aunt Jane herself.

Chapter 5

THE STORY OF THE AIR: PART 1

Many years ago there lived an old harper minstrel who travelled mostly around the North of Ireland though he visited the South and even went across to England and Scotland occasionally. He was renowned and welcomed everywhere for his music and his great skill as long as the Harp held sway. But its days, like those of himself were on the wane. Little by little this forced itself upon his attention in his wanderings, especially across the water where he found his beloved harp supplanted in the popular fancy by other musical instruments. Somewhat jealous and (?) resentful he eventually in search of solace made his way towards Maghera (pronounced MAR-he-RAR) in the county Londonderry. There he had always received a cordial welcome, great respect for his calling, and lavish hospitality. But here, of all places, the cold ugly truth was brought home to him beyond further question. He had to face the facts that not only was his own day over on account of his declining years and strength, but also that of his beloved Harp, ousted by the fiddle which he considered a noisy squealing usurper whose only merit lay in its lightness and portability. Here to his dismay he found that the old time welcome had somehow cooled off - the desire for his music was still there but the old time enthusiasm was absent. The hospitality alone was undiminished but he felt it was offered more for old time's sake than for anything else. It was a rude awakening and hurt his proud spirit so deeply that dejected, yet defiant, he decided to make his way at once into the Dungiven area where he knew he would find a more congenial, comforting atmosphere. The people in those remote parts were heart and soul with him in the things he loved and respected, and their inaccessibility rendered them safe from this wretched new fad. Accordingly he turned his face to the rough lonely road with his harp slung over his drooping and weary shoulders - he no longer could afford the usual attendant. Reaching the top of a long incline he sat down to rest - removing his harp and placing it unconsciously by force of habit between his knees as if about to play. Sitting thus and turning the past and the present over in his mind, disappointment, anger and resentment issued in a kind of defiance which savoured more of the will to win than a reluctant perversity. Little by little however the mental storm subsided and he fell to recalling the honours and glories of the past. Suddenly he awoke from his day dreaming to find his nimble fingers, seemingly of their own accord, drawing from the responsive strings a glorious melody, such as he had never composed or heard before. Wisely he relaxed and let them follow their own bent so to speak, sufficiently long for him to grasp something of the construction and rhythm of their theme. Then with determination he set about gleaning all available and committing it to his trained memory.

In the process he followed three steps or stages.

(1) Like a detached eavesdropper he listened to this flowing rippling stream of numerous notes all blending as they met - never a dissonant intruder amongst them.

(2) In this stream he perceived and noted certain dominant tones and intervals which he perceived if collected, selected and arranged in their self suggested order and emphasis would give harmonic sense and meaning to the whole.

(3) The final arrangement or allotting of the various tones to their self appointed order, restraint or emphasis. The completed whole emerging as a glorious Inspiration, almost a Battle Song, in as much as it stands carelessly at ease in its first movement, comes to attention gathering strength and direction in its second, and in its third steps forth bravely and irresistibly (?) to stimulate and uplift one of the noblest elements in human nature.

Having played it over several times for the sheer joy of it and to fix it indelibly in his memory he began to consider what he should do about it. A remnant of his wounded pride asserted itself and suggested that he should retrace his steps over the roads he had travelled in humiliation for months past and let them now hear what he could do - he and his harp might be less honoured than of old but they weren't finished with yet. On second thoughts however he felt that such a course would really lead nowhere and would only mean the lowering of himself, his art and this outcome of it - to him now a sacred trust.

Without further hesitations he slung his harp over his shoulders again and with renewed hope and strength he strode out in the closing day into the mountain wilds. There he decided he would deposit his "trust" in safe keeping, for observation and experience had taught him, if nothing else, that the hills can hold when the plains let go in travel or tradition. Slowly and methodically he traversed the area around those mountains particularly that to the east inclining North of Dungiven. He found no change in his reception here as he played some of the old familiar airs, and carefully, to the understanding ones alone imparted his masterpiece. To a favoured few (?) whose sympathy and self respect he knew he could trust he imparted his story of humiliation and uplift.

His remarks about the violin however, only served to rouse the curiosity of a negligible few who determined to get one as soon as he was out of the way, and did so, but on the whole his hearers were loyal to him and his harp. After a few years of this duty to his calling and himself he passed to his rest telling some shortly before he went how he felt he had not half finished his work. All things considered however, he had planted better than he knew (?). The marked intensity of his whole bearing towards that air, and his manner of playing it invested it with a mysterious something that touched even the dullest of his hearers. Somewhat awestricken they felt something out of the common was afoot and that they were privileged to share in a trust which they determined to keep among themselves for themselves and for safety sake.

Audley[21] dismisses this part of the story as "romanticised fiction", that had "purportedly" been told to Manning by his mother in a six page account". This is a sweeping dismissal from someone who had never seen the original papers. While this account, in its re-telling over the years, was doubtless subjected to the usual elaboration, there is nothing to suggest that Manning was relating anything other than his mother's words. In fact it reads like a bedtime story, as suggested by his description of her "measured mode" in recounting it.

Its description of the harper lamenting the decline in his fortunes is certainly suggestive of Dennis Hempson who was, as already noted, the last of the old style Irish harpers[39], and whose longevity ensured he outlived his popularity. As we have seen, he spent his later years in Magilligan, some twenty miles from Dungiven, and played "The Young Man's Dream", the acknowledged predecessor of "The Londonderry Air" to Edward Bunting in 1796. Bunting, however, found Hempson reluctant to play the old tunes since "they revived painful recollections"[3]. The decline of the harp and the corresponding rise in popularity of the violin became increasingly evident in the second half of the eighteenth century, but Dungiven was then and remains today a stronghold of the old Gaelic culture. The "east inclining" mountains "north of Dungiven" suggest the area around Benbradagh mountain.

It is interesting to note that the initial inspiration of the Air is said to have come in three contrasting versions, which corroborates Manning's description of his mother's interpretation in which she played it over "three times each different".

The most significant part of the Manning story now follows.

1. Canon W R F Manning (1878–1955)

2. Sophia Matilda Ross (1857–1914), daughter of Canon Ross and wife of William Manning

3.William Manning & Sophia Matilda Ross on their wedding day, the 20th July, 1876

4. Ballyorgan Church, Co Limerick

5. The interior of Ballyorgan Church

6. The Manning memorial in Ballyorgan Church

7. The Rev William Manning and his wife Alice French on their wedding day

8. The Rectory, Ballyorgan

9. Pete and Dagmar Smith

10. Jane Ross (1810--1879)

11. A mural of Jane Ross on the Main Street Limavady, with local legends

12. The Lodge Limavady as it is today

13. The Ross sisters' house in the Main Street, Limavady

14. The Ross family memorial in Christ Church graveyard

15. Christ Church Limavady

16. Sam Henry playing the tin whistle

17. Denis Hempson (c. 1695--1807)

18. Bunting's manuscript of "The Young Man's Dream"

19. Bunting's arrangement of "The Young Man's Dream" as copied into Theodosia Ross's manuscript book

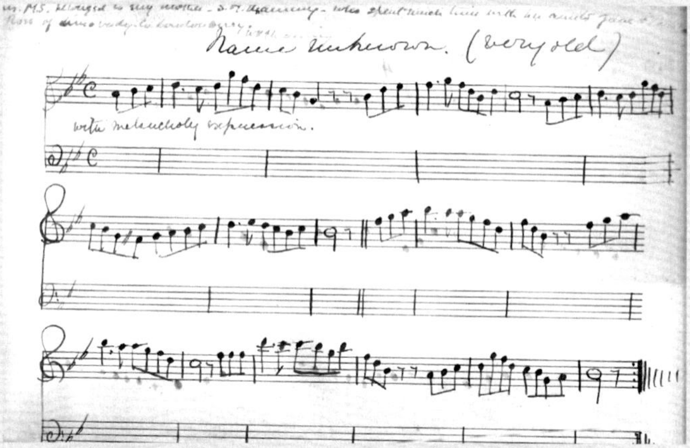

20. "The Londonderry Air" in the handwriting of Sophia Matilda Manning

21. Dungiven Parish Church Choir (c. 1877)

22. Canon William Ross (1814–1891),Vicar of Dungiven and brother of Jane Ross

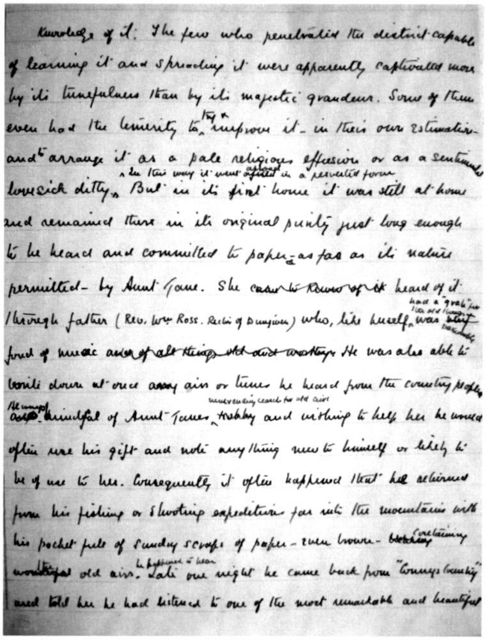

knowledge of it: The few who penetrated the district capable
of learning it and spreading it were apparently captivated more
by its tunefulness than by its majestic grandeur. Some of them
even had the temerity to try & improve it – in their own estimation –
and to arrange it as a pale religious effusion or as a sentimental
lovesick ditty, & in this way it went abroad in a perverted form.
But in its first home it was still at home
and remained there in its original purity just long enough
to be heard and committed to paper – as far as its nature
permitted – by Aunt Jane. She heard of it
through father (Rev. Wm Ross. Rector of Dungiven) who, like herself, had a "grab" for the old things & was [illegible]
fond of music [illegible] He was also able to
write down at once any air or tunes he heard from the country people.
He, [illegible] mindful of Aunt Jane's unwearying search for old airs and wishing to help her he would
often use his gift and note anything new to himself or likely to
be of use to her. Consequently it often happened that he returned
from his fishing or shooting expeditions far into the mountains with
his pocket full of sundry scraps of paper – even brown – containing
the old airs. It happened so when late one night he came back from "Cunnys Country"
and told her he had listened to one of the most remarkable and beautiful

23. A page from Canon Manning's account of the discovery of the Air

24. The earliest extant version of the Air, as it appears in Theodosia Ross's manuscript book

Chapter 6

THE STORY OF THE AIR: PART 2

There it (the Air) remained in security no doubt but in comparative obscurity which increased as the years went by narrowing the range and knowledge of it. The few who penetrated the district capable of learning and spreading it were apparently captivated more by its tunefulness than by its majestic grandeur. Some of them even had the temerity to try and improve it - in their own estimation and to arrange it as a pale religious effusion or as a sentimental lovesick ditty. In this way it went abroad in a perverted form. But in its first home it was still at home and remained there in its original purity just long enough to be heard and committed to paper as far as its nature permitted by Aunt Jane. She heard of it through father (Rev Wm. Ross, Rector of Dungiven) who like herself had a "grah" for the old things and was passionately fond of music. He was also able to write down at once any airs or tunes he heard from the country people. Always mindful of Aunt Jane's never ending search for old airs and wishing to help her he would often use his gift and note anything new to himself or likely to be of use to her. Consequently it often happened that he returned from his fishing or shooting expeditions far into the mountains with his pocket full of sundry scraps of paper - even brown - containing the old airs he happened to hear. Late one night he came back from "Connys Country" and told her he had listened to one of the most remarkable and beautiful tunes he had ever heard but was too pressed for time to stop and make his customary note of it. However, he whistled the first few bars of it for her and told her how to find the mountain cabin where he heard it played on a fiddle as he passed. More than interested Aunt Jane took the long drive from Limavady as soon as she could possibly manage it. Arriving at the cabin she found a very old man who received her with a reserve not unlike suspicion and showed little inclination to be communicative. However taking him gently she told him her name, where she had driven from, her hobby, how she had come to hear of the air she now wished to learn and make a note of, and ended by humming a few bars of it for him to recognise it. At once his whole attitude of aloofness changed as he told her he had heard tell of her love for the old music, also how good all the members of her family had been to the poor people suffering from famine and cholera. He went on to tell her how he heard father (Rev. W. Ross) went into a fever stricken house and carried out in his own arms a sick man when no-one else would go near him and put him in the fever cart to send him to hospital in hope of saving his life. Some time after when his Reverence got the fever himself the Roman Catholic Parish Priest assembled his flock in the chapel to pray for his recovery. Turning then to the air in question he told her the story of its coming to the old Harper, as already related. When he himself was a young man, he said, his father and several old men in the locality would meet and playing it over discuss its history, but they always seemed jealous about outsiders hearing it as if it were a great secret. Naturally, he remarked, their attitude infected him too and now that they were all gone he felt he alone knew it properly and his days were nearly over too. Deeply affected by his remembrance of the past he produced his fiddle of sorts for which he apologised saying a harp was of course the right instrument tho' he regretfully admitted he couldn't play one even if he could obtain it. With this foreword and seemingly conscious of the irony of the situation in view of the story he had related he did his best to play the air rendering it as he had got it from his father and the other old men. This simply consisted of playing the air three times over each differently in an effort to reproduce as far as the fiddle allowed, the three stages experienced by the old Harper as he gleaned it and fixed it in his memory on the road from Maghera.

Audley acknowledges this part of the story does have "a ring of truth" and "demands attention"[21]. Historically it fits well with the theory of Hempson being the harper. While the actual date of the event is not specified, it came after a time of famine and cholera which would suggest a date in the 1840s. If Jane Ross had heard the melody around that time from "a very old man" who had himself received it from his father, this would place the story in the second half of the eighteenth century when Hempson was indeed active.

The story of Canon Ross, Jane's brother, carrying a cholera victim to the fever cart is also historically accurate, being corroborated by a letter in the "Derry Sentinel" (a local paper) at the time of the Canon's death (1891) in which the Rev Robert Gage, a former curate of Limavady parish, recalls the incident as having occurred in the Canon's "twentieth year" (1834). (A copy of this letter may be found in the Manning papers).

The account of the Rev Ross suffering from "the fever" and being prayed for by the local Roman Catholics finds corroboration in his obituary in the same paper, (January 20th 1891) where it is said to have happened during his curacy in Maghera (1839-1847), and the fever to have been "famine fever".

The story of him first hearing the melody in "a mountain cabin" is also highly plausible. As Curate of Maghera and then Upper Cumber (1848-50), and Vicar of the neighbouring parish of Dungiven (from 1850)[40] he would have been surrounded by mountains, and would have passed many such "cabins" in the course of his work and leisure (photos 21 & 22).

The exact location of "Connys country" remains unclear, however (photo 23). There is no such townland. The local historian, Graham Mawhinney, has suggested it could refer to the Rev Thomas de Vere Coneys who had been curate of Sixtowns in the parish of Ballynascreen (the townland of Moneyconey, some ten miles south of Dungiven) from 1843 to 1845 when the Rev. Ross had been curate of the neighbouring parish of Maghera[41]. This seems a likely explanation. The Rev Ross might then have been travelling through the mountains around Dungiven to visit his sister in Limavady. And it would most certainly have been "a long drive from Limavady".

It should be noted that the Air is again described as having been played "three times over each differently".

Aunt Jane felt strangely moved by the whole incident so unexpected but concentrated all her thoughts and efforts on obtaining an accurate record of the air itself and the old man's rendering of it together with sufficient notes to enable her to expand it more fully on paper when she returned home. Fearing anything might escape her memory she did this at once and though not fully satisfied with the result she showed it to me telling me its story while playing it over for me knowing she must (?) love it all. She did not however write it in its fullness in her large MS collecting book contenting herself for the time being with its insertion in mere outline or unharmonised form until she had worked out a satisfying and comprehensive expansion of it together with the appropriate directions for the rendering of it as it had been rendered for her. This effort to make the whole complete caused her much anxiety and effort. - She would frequently go to the piano with a feeling she had got what she wanted and it would sound all right as she played but when put down in black and white it seemed inconclusive and unworthy. She would have been satisfied if she could have made the air tell its story and its message intelligibly on paper even half as well as that old man had made do (?) so on his wretched looking old fiddle. Time flew as she pursued her efforts to express on paper and in a manner intelligible to all and sundry what she had heard, and felt within herself to be a reality.

Presently a Dr. Petrie, a man well versed in Archaeology and old music, hearing of her called upon her. She gave him a great many airs that were new to him, but on this occasion she did not give him this air for two reasons: first she wanted to complete it with requisite directions for its true rendering; and secondly she wanted to consider and decide how she stood as regards the publication of this air which seemed to have been given her in implied confidence and she could not help feeling something of the mysterious atmosphere and secrecy surrounding it. Later on feeling partly that she could not do all she wanted about the air and in deference to his unquestionable ability and enthusiasm and hoping he would perhaps succeed where she had failed she sent it to him with the simple inscription "Name unknown - very old". The only directions for its rendering she felt safe at the moment in giving were, for the first few bars "with melancholy". This was the atmosphere surrounding its inception, and its reception by herself, and she hoped that the playing of the first part of it in this manner would in itself engender a natural and appropriate reaction for the last part and by this means promote in some degree its proper rendering and spirit.

Dr. Petrie did not respond in the manner she expected as he published it as a piano piece with the complimentary harmonies filled in - technically correct no doubt, but far short of the real thing.

Disappointed and not knowing what to do to correct this miscalculation Aunt Jane worked away endeavouring to give the air as she got it and to retrieve this awkward situation. She had not succeeded to her satisfaction up to the time I left Dungiven (1876) and I am afraid she died leaving it unfinished as I could never find it in completed form any time I went back home and it is only in skeleton (?) outline in her large MS book I have here.

It should now be clear that Jane Ross was never satisfied with her attempt to notate the Air, and laboured on at it for the rest of her life, "seeking a satisfying and comprehensive expansion" of what she had been able to copy down of the old man's playing. For this reason, and in respect to the "implied confidence" with which it had been entrusted to her, she did not give it to Petrie on his visit to her house. His publication of it as a piano piece was a disappointment, and "far short of the real thing".

There the story ended for that day, but the impression Mother left on my mind was that she felt in some degree at least the publishing of the true rendering of this air now devolved upon her, and in later conversations with her she expressed the intention of doing so herself and refused offers of help from several whose zeal she thought outweighed their qualifications. Temperamental and otherwise I would often hear her playing it on the piano and several times on a church organ. I remember she used it once as an outgoing voluntary but the congregation --- (?). She played it most frequently however on an instrument which she loved perhaps for its approximate (?) harp like tone, an old guitar of exceptional carrying power and sweetness which had belonged to a great uncle and was sent home with his other effects after he was killed at the storming of Badajoz in the Peninsular War. She often told me of her wish to complete, as well as she could, the unfinished aim of her aunt but the time and opportunity for the requisite undivided attention never came before she herself passed away suddenly and unexpectedly twenty-two years ago (1914). A few years later when going through her piles of music, MS and others (?) I came across several efforts in her writing to put this air in its fullness on paper but they were corrected and re-corrected and none completed. Knowing she would not wish it go forth in this ragged form and not knowing into what unsympathetic hands her labour of love might fall in the indiscriminate --- (?) and looting in those troubled years I burned them. As a matter of fact the house containing them was raided several times for no apparent reason other than a flair for destruction and it may have happened that Aunt Jane's large MS book was taken or destroyed by those irresponsible patriots. Anyhow I could not find it though I deliberately went to look for it expecting it to be there, as Mother had told me a few years before her death that she had lent it to someone but was getting it back. Whether she did so or not I am unable to say and have no means of ascertaining now. However from the wreckage I rescued the MS book of my Aunt Theodosia a sister of Aunt Jane and a willing tho' less qualified helper in her folk music hobby. In Miss Theodosia Ross's MS book the Air appears thus: (photo 24).

Manning's mother continued her aunt's attempts to reconstruct the Air in its original form and style. In her manuscript version (photo 20) the faint outline of such efforts may still, in fact, be seen. Why her son felt it necessary to destroy these attempts remains a mystery. His explanations, for once, lack credibility. And what of Jane's own attempted reconstructions? Did they suffer a similar fate? And what became of her MS book? It had been in his mother's house "a few years before her death" in 1914. Had it never been returned by the person to whom she lent it? Or was it destroyed by "irresponsible patriots"? But if so, why was hers taken and Theodosia's MS book overlooked? Sophia Matilda Manning's death was registered in Navan. According to Pete Smith she would then have been living nearby in Kells. Could Jane's MS book still survive in the attic of some ancient residence in that area? Who can tell. As it is, Theodosia's version of the Air remains the earliest MS version we possess. It is not identical with Petrie's, however, differing in the last three notes of the fourth bar - a fact that has hitherto gone unnoticed. How did this happen? Many questions remain.

Chapter 7

FURTHER REFLECTIONS OF CANON WILLIAM MANNING

This chapter contains some of Manning's notes and reflections on the subject of the Air. Since they were not intended for public consumption they may appear disorganised and repetitive; however, they do cast further light on his motives, and in places, provide some additional interesting information.

Difficulty of putting Irish music in writing shown in J. McDonnell's letter to Bunting where he says: "Be sure to explain fully your own ideas as a musician and a philosophical reasoning man about the whole subject, and endeavour to show how it happens that other musicians, although expert and learned in their art never are able to play a Scotch or Irish air with any effect by any mode yet discovered of committing them to writing".

Had I read these words before (1936) I put my recollections on paper some with an effort to suggest the original rendering of this air as I heard it long ago I don't think I would have penned all this even though I should have felt a deeper sense of duty shirked more even than I do now for my years of silence. However, I now commit all to print with the hope that someone with a "grah" for these things and the spirit that prompted Aunt Jane in her collection, and qualified to do so, may successfully express in musical notation something more of the Harper composer's spirit and inspiration than I can feel I have lamely (?) done in words which at best can only half reveal and half conceal or as my mother put it "There are no words to it; there never could be".

This indicates that Manning's intention in writing his account was the hope that someone in the future might be able to put on paper a version of the Air that corresponded more to what his great-aunt Jane had originally heard - a task that would, of course, have been greatly simplified had he not destroyed his mother's attempted reconstructions.

Composer of the Londonderry Air

O'Carolan

Pro: Often heard him mentioned by mother, also others,
Con: but Carolan seldom, if ever, visited the North.

Denis Hempson

Pro: While mother never told me definitely as far as I can remember the name of the old Harper to whom the air came on the road from Maghera yet I often heard her speak of "Old Hempsey the Harper". Looking up the various lists of known Harpers I can find no name Hempsey but I find one very like it, namely Denis Hempson. Considerable details of his life and outlook I find in a book recently recommend(ed) to me "Annals of the Irish Harpers" by Charlotte Milligan Fox. Now chapter XII the following facts can be gathered which afford a reasonable presumption that Hempson (was) the composer.

(1) He was born in 1695 (died 1807) in Co. Londonderry, Craigmore, near Garvagh.

(2) Travelled through Ireland and over the Sea.

(3) In old age (he) settled down at Magilligan strand in his native territory and not a two days journey from Limavady and district.

(4) Intolerant of modern music and delighted in the most antiquated he could find.

(5) Remarkable for his staccato playing (Bunting deeply impressed by his execution. Much of this in the rendering I am trying to express).

(6) Lost his sight at three but bravely conquered the defect.

(7) A man of courage and sensitive, intelligent (?) possessed fine feeling.

(8) Did not play the "Londonderry Air" for Rev. Sampson as one would have expected in view of the story of it, (Rev. Sampson's letter 1805), or if he did the Rev. Sampson did not take the particular note of it one would have expected - Rev. S. simply says he played his favourite tunes and then the ones Rev. S. had to ask for. "Coolin" etc.

From letter we learn that his last days were rendered comfortable by Rev. Sir H. Harvey Bruce. The day before his death on hearing that this gentleman had come to his cabin he desired to be raised up in his bed, and the harp placed in his hands. Having struck some notes of a favourite strain, he sank back unable to proceed, taking his last adieu. (Was this an effort to impart to a kind benefactor his great (?) inspiration and the effort and excitement produced a tension his heart was not able to stand?)

The conclusion of the Rev. Sampson's letter very significant and almost word for word with the story told by the old man in the Sperrin Mountain Cabin to Aunt Jane. "When asked" the letter concludes "to play the very antique tunes he uniformly (?) replied. "There was no use in doing so, they were too hard to learn, they revived painful recollections! In short he regarded the old music with a superstitious veneration and thought it in some sort a profanation to divulge it to modern ears." Compare this with that part of the story which says - "the hills can hold" etc.

Temperament, disposition, incidents of close of his life all give a reasonable presumption that Hempson is the Author.

Bunting visited him but found him uncommunicative.

Unless and until I get more direct and concrete evidence of some other composer of this air I shall hold that Hempson was the one to whom it came out of the blue on the slopes of Carntogher.

This is a closely reasoned and well researched reflection which comes to the conclusion that the harper of the story was, indeed, Denis Hempson. It could even be that the "Old Hempsey" to whom his mother referred was simply "O'Hampsey", the Irish version of his name.

We shall never know if there was indeed "staccato" playing in his mother's rendition of the Air as Manning implies, but he correctly notes the similarity in sentiment between the harper of the story and the words of Hempson, as quoted in the Rev Sampson's letter of 1805[39].

Reasons for Silence.

"It is a natural desire in the majority of men to keep a secret garden in their souls, a something that they do not care to talk about, still less to set down, for the other members of the herd to trample on." So wrote "Don Roberto" (R. B. Cunninghame Graham) in his book, "Writ in Sand". Partly for this reason, and partly from the fear of being misunderstood, and mostly from a sense of lack of qualifications, literary and musical, to do justice to my subject that I kept to myself what I knew of the origin and interpretation of the so called "Londonderry Air". But some little time ago a friend kindly permitted me a hasty glance at his copy of Bunting in which I read in the preface . . . . .

I felt the force of these words at once and agreed with them and found myself confronted with the conflict between Inclination and Duty ---. But I remembered a hearing of my University lecture on mental and moral philosophy saying one day: "When two courses are open to you, each fair and right and you are in doubt which to adopt, then follow the harder one!"

So I take up my pen and limp down the path to open the gate that leads to one of the flower pots in my garden.

This section expands on the reasons for his long silence - namely his fear of publicity, and his lack of literary and musical qualifications. It seems to have taken some considerable effort for him to overcome these doubts. R B Cunninghame Graham was a Scottish Socialist, and also a famous adventurer. The Bunting quotation to which he alludes is presumably that which began his account in chapter 4.

Jane Ross

Miss Jane Ross, lineal descendant of John Ross, Burgess of Limavady, lived on some of the property there inherited from him. Born in 1810 she was the eldest of a family of six - a responsible position in those days - and eventually when, in the usual course of events the family grew up and scattered she was enabled to devote more time to her then unique hobby of collecting and playing all the old folk music she could find. A lover of accuracy she made a point of collecting from those who in her judgement were best qualified to impart an air in its original form. This hobby she had pursued since girlhood but was able to expand more fully and comprehensively in the famine and cholera years owing to the close intercourse and intimacy afforded in those dark days to anyone whose charitable nature brought them in contact with hungry wanderers or carried them far afield into out of the way places to seek and relieve distress. Soon her collection expanded beyond the possibility of keeping it tidy and easy of reference so she procured a large MS book with her name inscribed in gilt lettering on the outside and into this she inserted no air until she believed she had obtained (it) in their correct original and she was satisfied that she had exhausted all choices (?) open to her to ensure that she had it as nearly as she could get it to its original form. She also procured a similar book for her admiring though less capable sister Theodosia. Mother had both books but Aunt Jane's is now missing. However Theodosia's which I have before me as I write contains several hitherto unpublished airs --- (?), also this air in its skeleton or unharmonised form and doubtless so copied by her from Jane's book. Comparing it with Petrie's publication, also before me, both are . . . . .

My great Aunt Jane inserted in a fairly thick handsomely bound MS book all the Irish airs she could collect herself from the various sources open to her and as far as I remember included some that she particularly liked from the already printed collections of others working in the same field. Mother had this book and I remember her telling me she had lent it to somebody but would get it back. Whether she did so or not I cannot say but I could find no trace of it after her death and fear it may have perished or fallen into unappreciati(ve) hands in a senseless raid on the house by some irresponsibles who took advantage of the troubled state of the country to indulge their looting propensities or display their Iberian origin in its love of destroying for destruction's sake. On subsequent (?) I could only find the incomplete efforts to set forth the proper (?)

study of this air which I destroyed for the reasons given and retained my great Aunt Theodosia's MS book, sister of Jane and resident with her.

. . . . The book is dimension (?) part leather and marbled paper covered with "Theodosia" inscribed in gilt lettering on a small rectangular leather tab affixed to the outer cover.

In this book the Air appears thus just as it did in its skeleton or unharmonised form in Aunt Jane's book, a duplicate though thicker.

This is the most revealing account we have of the life of Jane Ross. The statement that "she lived on some of the property" she inherited from her father is corroborated, as noted, in the 1858 Griffith's Valuation where a "Jane Ross" is listed as the lessor of a number of properties in central Limavady. The oft repeated claim that she was a "teacher" or "piano teacher" has, therefore, no foundation in fact. As the eldest daughter she played a part in the rearing of her younger siblings before devoting herself to her hobby of collecting all the old tunes she could find, a hobby she pursued through the years of famine. Her devotion to this hobby must, therefore, have dated from around 1840. She was a lover of accuracy and inserted no Air into her large MS book until she was satisfied it was correct. This book also included melodies she particularly liked from other printed collections. Its fate, as we have seen, remains a mystery.

Whether the version of the Air in Jane's book was identical with that of her sister (as Manning claims), thus differing in three notes from Petrie's printed version, we cannot now tell.

The Air and the Old Harper

The irony of it - the old man recognised it and seemed rather ashamed that he had to play it on a fiddle for want of a harp. She felt she should not break his confidence indirectly given her, therefore related story to none except beloved niece = mother. Withheld it from Dr P. - did not even give him tune on his visit but reluctantly later in respect to his marked ability in 1st. vol. 1853 sent it to him marked "Name unknown, very old, with sympathy" (sic) - a wide term - what more could she do but leave it to his educated instincts to expand it and publish it to the best effect. But he published just as given and there it remains until someone takes it up and print(s) it appropriately in the light of its history.

These are significant reflections, though written on an envelope and difficult to decipher. Jane Ross revealed the story of the Air to no-one, except her "beloved niece", Manning's mother. She did not give the melody to Petrie when he visited, but only sent it to him with reluctance after the initial publication in 1853 of some of the items of his subsequent volume of 1855[21]. Did she describe to him the three contrasting versions with which it was played to her? We shall never know, but he did not "expand it" as she had hoped.

Chapter 8

CORRESPONDENCE

The Manning papers include a number of letters from relations and researchers. These are now included with comments, as appropriate.

Correspondence with the Rev. J. T. Trelawny-Ross

Manning writes:

In the issue of the "Northern Whig" Belfast dated August 21/1928 there appeared the following letter written by my uncle, my mother's eldest brother, the Rev. J. T. Trelawny Ross D.D. TCD.

Sir,

A friend has sent me a cutting from your paper, and with your leave I will give what I believe to be the true story of the discovery and saving of the air. Let me clear up two statements, both of which were made in an English paper a few days ago.

(1) That the late Miss Honoria Galwey "about 50 years ago" (say 1878) heard the air in Limavady, jotted it down, and took it to the late Canon Armstrong, and that thus it "was rescued from oblivion". But George Petrie published it in 1855, 23 years before this rescue.

(2) The statement by Mr. Alfred Percival Graves that a "Miss Anna Ross" had collected the air for Petrie. Evidence already points to the air having been rescued by a Miss Ross, of Limavady. But the only Anna Ross in Limavady for at least the last 229 years was the wife of my cousin William Stewart Ross of Barley Park. He died in 1890. She was not a musician.

There is every reason for believing that the finder and preserver of the Air was my eldest Aunt, Miss Jane Ross, who was born at the Lodge Limavady 1810, and died 1879. Her father was John Ross, who commanded the Limavady Yeomanry, horse and foot. On the passing of the Union Lord Londonderry, Custos Rotulorum, handed over to him all the muniments, seal and corporation Records of the dissolved borough. My father, Canon Ross, kept them safely, and they are here awaiting a safe Government home in Ulster.

My aunt was well known, not only as a collector, but for her delightful piano playing of all kinds of old Irish music, not least reels and dance music. They were stored in her memory. Often as I have heard her play never once did I see a page of music on the piano. She probably took her collection of old Irish music to Petrie about 1853 when I was an infant. I well remember one of her MS books, wherein was a realistic musical description of a fox hunt. I know nothing about the fiddler, or possibly piper from whose playing she took down the Air.

Four years ago I had a talk with my friend the Dean of Derry. He alluded to my Aunt's visit to Petrie, and told me that Lord Shaftesbury wished greatly to know the whereabouts of the rest of her collection. I thought that it might be here, but a thorough search has yet to be made.

Yours etc.
J. T. Trelawny-Ross. D.D.
Ham, near Plymouth,
August 16. 1928

Manning adds:

Since the publication of that letter I have had several letters and talks with my uncle about the matter. He was unaware, when we first discussed the subject, that Dr. Petrie in his volume of 1855 in a note page 57 acknowledged the receipt of the air from Miss Jane Ross, nor did he know until I told him my mother's account of the circumstances under which Jane R. gave Dr. Petrie that air or how according to the same account she, Jane Ross "discovered" it.

The Rev. J. T. Trelawny-Ross's letter was the first public statement from a member of the Ross family on the subject of the Air. It corrects the errors that had recently been appearing in newspaper correspondence, and provides some interesting personal details about his aunt, as he remembers her.

It does appear to be the limit of his knowledge, however, as Manning notes at the end of the letter. This fact should always be remembered when considering some of the comments of his descendants, who did not know Jane Ross.

As from Ham, near Plymouth
July 20/1932

My dear Joe,

Just a line to thank you humbly for all that you have kindly done - we have the Teignworth family with us at present - I have filled up the enclosed and will write further thereon when I can. I have tax bothers, owing to the carelessness of the officials here, and the war loan conversion has given me a lot of trouble.

Bunting's second volume was bound with the first, at the British Museum. I read the Preface, and saw no mention of any Ross. The book was published in

1796, and my Aunt Jane was not born till well into the next century. I expect that the second volume came at some time later. I don't think there was any preface to it; but it may have been taken out by the binder. I was glad to hear what you said about the "Londonderry Air" and a harper. I have come to a conviction that it was composed for only a harper; and that on other grounds. I am very glad to hear that you have it in Aunt Theodosia's book. I copied the air as it is in Bunting's book (sic), and there are certain notes marked for accenting, to make them clear and prominent.

Parry is quite a broken man; or, I am afraid was; C. V. Stanford, like Parry, thought highly of the air.

Best love to you all. "Quosque (?) tandem" in Ireland?

Ever your affectionate nephew (sic),

J. T. Trelawny-Ross

The "Joe" to whom this letter was addressed was, of course, Canon Manning himself who was affectionately known by this name. The letter seems a little confused - as regards Bunting - and in his signing of himself as "affectionate nephew", but it is interesting to note that he had come to the conclusion the Air was composed for a harper.

Manning's questions to his uncle now follow. His uncle's replies are in italics:

"Who were the Misses Ross who supplied Petrie* (see his preface) with many of his Irish Airs - name their father or mother?" (*Originally Bunting).

"None of the name mentioned in the Preface. Read it the other day. A Society in Belfast employed Bunting to meet gatherings of harpers, and take down their old airs - 2 vols. published in 1796".

"Name of father or mother of Jane Ross who gave the "Londonderry Air" to Petrie?"

"John Ross, married (2) Jane Ogilby, your great grandfather".

"Have you any music amongst the boxes etc I think you showed me as having come to you from Dungiven or Limavady?"

"Nothing, I am afraid, of value".

"What instruments were played by Jane Ross above mentioned?"

"Piano".

"Have you any information as to how or when Jane Ross obtained this Air?"

"She took it down from a wandering musician, and sent it with other airs to Petrie in time for the publication of his Volume of Ancient Irish Music 1855".

"Mother told me that Jane Ross or some member of her family had the faculty

of being able to note down immediately on paper any air sung or whistled for them and got many thus in their travels in Donegal and elsewhere - is there any foundation for this?"
"Aunt Jane must have had knowledge enough of music to take down an air from a harper or violinist etc."

I think that there is another air published, in addition to "Danny Boy" - I remember her MS book well - it had in it a descriptive piece, the "Fox Hunt".

Please write soon and tell me what you have got. If it be the collection, I will ask you to send it over to me, that I may get expert advice. It might be the means of great financial help to you. The Band Master of the Marines Band is one of three famous Irish brothers, all Band Masters.

I hope that you all are well. I have had no rest for nearly 3 years, and "the unexpected" and fresh duties appear regularly.

Toto (?) gives a gloomy account of matters. Best love to you all.

Ever your affectionate Uncle,

J. T. Trelawny-Ross.

The Rev J. T. Trelawny-Ross's replies to Manning's questions are illuminating. Writing in 1932 he could state that no music had come to Ham house from Dungiven or Limavady. He clearly had no more idea than anyone else about the fate of his Aunt Jane's MS book. Had these facts been known the subsequent searches of Ham House would have been unnecessary. Toto was Canon Manning's youngest brother, Robert.

Correspondence with D. J. O'Sullivan

Cairn Hill,
Foxrock,
County Dublin
20th July, 1932.

Dear Mr Manning,

Very many thanks for your long and interesting letter of the 16th instant. I shall be delighted to see you when you are passing through Dublin at the end of the month and to look at Theodosia Ross's manuscript, as well as to get any other information you are able to give me. You might drop me a card in advance telling me the day and time you will call in at the Senate, so that I shall be there.

As regards your queries, Bunting's first volume, entitled Ancient Music of Ireland *(sic), was published in 1796. The "Londonderry Air" was first published by Dr. George Petrie in his Ancient Music of Ireland which appeared in 1855. I do not know off-hand the date of Parry's book but it is not important since Parry and everyone else who has used or arranged the air has taken it, directly or indirectly, from Petrie. There is no other independent printed source of the air whatever. I am not well acquainted with any modern harpist, nor do I think it would be quite practicable for you to try to impart to any harpist your recollection of the way your mother played this tune. It would be far better, in my opinion, for you to work the thing out at the piano and to get your little daughter to help you note the tune according to your recollection. You could then make her play it for you from her notation and have it altered until it is quite in accordance with your recollection. It is very important for us to have such a notation if we are to do some research work on the tune in a satisfactory manner.*

I was delighted to meet you and I look forward to seeing you again at the end of the month.

With kind regards and every good wish.

I remain,
Yours sincerely,
D. J. O'Sullivan

This letter from the scholarly D. J. O'Sullivan indicates Manning's wish, even at that time, to reconstruct the Air in the manner he had heard his mother play it. O'Sullivan, however, was clearly unaware of Manning's destruction of his mother's attempted reconstructions.

Letter from D. J. O'Sullivan on his receipt of Theodosia Ross's MS book:

Cairn Hill,
Foxrock,
County Dublin
2nd August, 1932.

Dear Mr Manning,

Many thanks for your letter and for the MS. book, both of which arrived by hand this morning. If you handed them in personally I am sorry you did not drop up to have a word with me. Unfortunately, there is not a single tune in the MS. which is not copied from a printed book. Practically all the Irish ones are copied from one or other of Bunting's three volumes. The copy of the "Londonderry Air" looks to me on a cursory glance to be identical with the tune as published by Petrie, but without having both copies in front of me at the same time I could not be sure. The musical description of the fox hunt which you believe to have been in Jane Ross's book was perhaps copied from one of the earlier printed books which contain it.

I am keeping the MS in my room in the Senate in case you call tomorrow morning. The MS book of Joyce's is in the possession of my friend Dr. R. D. Joyce of Merrion Square. I shall try and get it on loan for you some time, but at the moment I am up to my eyes in work on account of the political situation.

With kind regards,

I remain,
Yours sincerely,
D. J. O'Sullivan

This letter is informative in that it gives the verdict of an acknowledged expert on Theodosia's MS book - the tunes had all been copied from earlier printed books, mostly by Bunting! It is interesting to note, however, that his "cursory glance" failed to detect that her version of "The Londonderry Air" was not, in fact, identical with Petrie's.

Correspondence from Miss Anne Gilchrist
Part of a letter to Canon Manning:

Walnut Bank,
Lancaster,
October 29th 1932

Dear Mr Manning

Thank you very much for your kind and most interesting reply. Your reminiscences of your mother's playing of the air as distinct from the written copy may prove a confirmation of my theory - at any rate I am going to try the experiment and see whether your recollection at all bears out my notion of how the tune was intended to be sung and played. It is a sad pity that I couldn't just come and see you, and hear you give it in your mother's way! But at any rate I can send you the tune as I imagine it may have been performed, and you will be able to tell me if it is anything like what you remember.

Of course the problem of the tune is its absence of words, for it is obviously a ballad-air; and my idea is that all the words which have been written to it since it was printed by Petrie falsify its metre and rhythm, but that it did fit a well-known Irish stanza called Ochtfochlech bec (Mr O'Sullivan named it for me) --- . -------------------------------------.

Well, now I include my theoretical restoration and hope very much that it may not be altogether wrong. But I hope nevertheless that you may be able to transfer your impressions and Mrs Manning's "way of it" to someone nearer at hand than I am! - and I shall await your kind reply with a keen anticipation and hope of clearing up the mystery surrounding the beautiful air - which some people think too beautiful to be a real folk song at all! - but perhaps that is just jealousy on the Sassenach's part! With many thanks

Yours sincerely,
Anne G. Gilchrist

Miss Gilchrist was clearly interested in a reply Canon Manning had sent her in that it could have confirmed her theory that the Air should have been written in triple time. Unfortunately there was no convenient way of confirming this possibility.

Letter from D. J. O'Sullivan concerning Miss Anne Gilchrist's article:

Cairn Hill,
Foxrock,
County Dublin.
1st February, 1936.

Dear Mr Manning,

I was very pleased to hear from you again. The particulars you ask for will be found on the first page of the enclosed little off-print from the Journal of the English Folk Dance and Song Society. I shall be glad if you will let me have this back when you are quite done with it and if you would like a copy yourself I shall write to Miss Gilchrist and get you one. I am particularly anxious to hear whether the way Miss Gilchrist suggests the tune should be played (as printed on page 119) is at all like the way you heard it from your mother.

I hope you will drop in to see me for a chat at the Senate some time when you come to Dublin.

With kind regards,

I remain,
Yours sincerely,
D. J. O'Sullivan

D. J. O'Sullivan was clearly impressed by Miss Gilchrist's theory to which, as related in her letter, he had contributed, but Canon Manning was not able to answer his query.

Correspondence with the Rev. W.T. Trelawny-Ross
(Son of the Rev. J.T. Trelawny-Ross)

Ham, near Plymouth
February 2, 1939

Dear Joe,

Many thanks for yours of Jan. 30th. I wrote to Mr Sam Henry, of Coleraine, as he was the man who had told Mr A. Doherty the name of the fiddler in Limavady, and I have had the gist of his reply typed. I send you a copy. I wonder if he is to be relied on. Doherty to whom I wrote, quoting part of Dad's letter in the "Northern Whig", August 21, 1928, replied that he was deeply interested in the facts which I had sent him and considered my letter of such importance that he was taking the liberty of publishing part of it ("what ho", she cried, and waved her wooden leg!) !! and now he wants at my convenience, any other biographical details about Miss Jane Ross. If only I had been going over to Ireland, as I had hoped, the week after next, I would have gone and seen dear old Miss Cather, one of Dad's oldest friends, at Limavady, as Sam Henry says that she remembers Aunt Jane well. He, by the way, has a beautiful photograph of Miss Ross. I would dearly like to see him, too. Lady Londonderry has just written beautiful new words for the Air.*

I wish you would send me a copy of what you have written about it. You say you have the main history written - the circs. in which it was composed and how aunt Jane found it - "and now I want to say a little about aunt Jane herself ------------- " (this is quoted from your letter of 17/7/1937 to me).

With love to you and Dolly

Ever yours,
Willie.

The remainder of the letter concerns family history including:

This was the list of names which I had inscribed in lead on the Head block in Limavady Churchyard -

"In Memory of

John Ross	*1778-1830*
Theodosia Ross	*1819-1875*
Jane Ross	*1810-1879*
Elizabeth Ross	*1812-1889*
Caroline Matilda Ross	*1817-1889*
Canon William Ross	*1814-1891*

and other members of the Ross family resting in this Churchyard".

*** Extracts from a letter written on 26 January 1939 to the Rev. W. T. Trelawny-Ross by Mr Sam Henry, Sandelford, Coleraine, Co Londonderry:**

The Londonderry Air

The strong local tradition is that a fiddler, named John McCormick, played the tune in the street opposite the Alexander Arms Hotel, Limavady. Miss Jane Ross then lived in the other street. She heard the tune, took the fiddler in, gave him hospitality, and learnt it.

I got a spontaneous letter from a man in Toronto who said that he owned the fiddle on which the air was played to Miss Ross at that time. He bought it from McCormick's son at Ballymena. Many people remember a travelling show called McCormick's show. It was a feature in the small towns in the County Londonderry about 50 years ago (1889) and earlier. A grandson of the John McCormick is still fiddling in the Ulster fairs. I tried to get in touch with him but failed.

I have collected "The Londonderry Air" independently, and a fine variant of it was collected in Chicago from Irish people by O'Neill, whose collection of Irish Airs is superb.

I have gone into the origin of the air and am convinced that it was composed by Rory Dall O'Cahan, harper to the O'Neill. He went to Scotland and at least 8 of his compositions are known. Its theme is the glory and eclipse of the O'Cahan Clan at the Plantation of Ulster. No words accompanied it. My Toronto correspondent said that the fiddler told him that the air was just one of Rory O'Cahan's tunes.*

It was a characteristic of Rory's music that he avoided the sub-dominant note F. In the Chicago version this note does not occur.

* The Rev. W. T. Trelawny-Ross adds:
Mrs Milligan Fox may have been the authority for this conviction on the part of Mr Sam Henry - or vice versa! Rory Dall O'Cahan flourished about 500 years ago. The great Irish Chieftain was Hugh O'Neill.

Canon Manning comments:
This Air was little known until long after Petrie's publication of it. Aunt Jane was interested in any old airs she heard and it would require very clear evidence to assert that when she heard McCormick playing, it was definitely the Londonderry Air, and even if it was it is not outside the range of possibility that being already in possession of the air, as related by her niece, and wondering what she should do about it, she simply invited McCormick into her house in order to ascertain his knowledge of its origin and interpretation.

The Rev. W. T. Trelawny-Ross understandably knew much less about Jane Ross and the Air than his father, and was troubled by the letter he had received from Sam Henry, the local journalist and broadcaster. Well might he comment "I wonder if he is to be relied on".

Here he is introduced to the legend of the street musician, a fiddler named McCormick, and a harper named Rory Dall O'Cahan, on the basis of a "strong local tradition" - a convenient term, beloved of folklorists, which as usual is neither quantified nor evaluated. The Rev. W. T. Trelawny-Ross's perplexity, and that of his cousin, is apparent, but their response to these surprising revelations was measured and polite.

In questioning the reliability of Henry's "research" the Rev W. T. Trelawny-Ross was not, of course, to be alone. As Hugh Shields was to comment forty years later it usually needed to be "digested with a grain of salt"[31] (footnote 13)!

Correspondence from Hugh Shields

Part of a letter from Hugh Shields to Mrs P. Smith (daughter of Canon Manning) concerning Miss Theodosia Ross's MS. book:

University of Dublin,
French department,
3 June 1989

Dear Mrs Smith,

---------------------------------. I have not discovered anything from any other source about the "Londonderry Air" since we last discussed it. What I found about the manuscript was that
(1) It does not throw much light on that particular tune but is most interesting as a contemporary copy of it which was in the Ross family, and
(2) It contains a lot of other tunes which include ones I was unable to trace elsewhere and perhaps actually unpublished. It is always difficult to be sure of such a thing, as I found in studying Canon J. Goodman's 19th century collection (in Trinity library) - in which, however, I was interested to find that he had copied the "Londonderry Air" out of Petrie's volume (that would have been some time in the 1860s. ---.

With best wishes
Hugh Shields

By now Canon Manning was long since dead. His daughter, however, was continuing the family quest. She had lent Hugh Shields who was, as we have seen, an acknowledged expert on the music of the Limavady area, her father's papers on the subject, and Theodosia Ross's MS book. His verdict on Theodosia's book was polite rather than encouraging. Unlike D. J. O'Sullivan he was unable to locate the source of all her tunes. He photocopied, but did not pursue the Manning account of the Air's discovery.

Chapter 9

CONCLUSIONS

The words of the Canon W. R. F. Manning have now been given the publicity they deserve, and which he intended. His account of the Air's discovery is very different from the myths and misinformation that are usually associated with the melody and may still be found, not least on the internet. It is up to the reader to decide on its veracity and significance.

For my part, I find Canon Manning a reliable witness, and his account an honest and convincing record of what he was told by his mother. When one studies his notes a person of integrity emerges who is trying to make sense of the knowledge with which he had been entrusted, and is seeking the appropriate course of action. He was not prone to exaggeration or speculation. If anything, he was too was aware of his limitations. His account is not over complimentary to the memory of Jane Ross, and makes no attempt to conceal the difficulties and disappointments she endured in her attempts to reconstruct the famous melody. For these reasons I find it a compelling and accurate chronicle of what he knew. As such it forms the only written record we possess of the true origins and development of this most famous of Irish melodies.

There is nothing in his account that can be shown to be historically inaccurate, and much of the detail can be verified from other sources. This is especially so with his story of the harper on the road from Maghera to Dungiven. Far from being "romanticised fiction", this fits well with the known facts of the life of Denis Hempson, the last of the Irish harpers of the old Gaelic tradition. His own words, as reported at the end of his long life[39], regretted the passing of the older musical style of his youth. What would have been more natural, therefore, than for him to express this regret in his music, and to base it on "The Young Man's Dream", which we know he played, and which remains the acknowledged forerunner of "The Londonderry Air"? His decision to entrust his inspiration to musicians in Dungiven was consistent with its reputation as an area where the older traditions remained strong.

Another indication the harper of the story was indeed Hempson is the statement that the harper had visited Scotland. Hempson is known to have been particularly popular in that country and played there to Bonny Prince Charlie in 1745[38].

Further proof of the veracity of the account is provided by the story of the Rev Ross and the cholera victim which was still remembered, as we have seen, nearly sixty years later at the time of his death. The story of his recovery from "the fever" after being prayed for by the local Roman Catholic congregation was also factually correct.

The stated form of the composition is of particular interest. It consisted of three versions of the melody, each different in expression. In musical terms it was a set of variations, a form Hempson had encountered in the arrangements of the harper, Lyons, which he played to Bunting in Magilligan. This would explain the statement of Canon Manning's mother that "It has no name and there are no words to it - there never could be," and would also account for Jane Ross's uninspiring title of "Name Unknown". It would also explain the respect with which it was viewed by those few who were aware of its existence. This was no ordinary melody to be played at the usual social occasions!

Hempson's involvement would, of course, vindicate her statement that the melody was "very old". If she had copied it from an elderly fiddler, who had learnt it from his father, who had in turn received it from Denis Hempson who only played the melodies of his youth, it must have been an ancient tune!

Jane Ross's problems with the notation of the melody, and her unwillingness to betray the confidence that had been entrusted to her by the fiddler, explain one of the abiding mysteries of the Air - her reason for not giving it to Petrie when he called at her home, along with the other tunes she provided at that time. Had she discussed her dilemma with him, the result might have been very different. Had he not warned that harpers and others instrumentalists "were usually the least to be trusted" because of the "barbarous licences" with which they interpreted the melodies[2]? It was hardly his fault when the printed version of her Air turned out "far short of the real thing".

While the Manning papers give a coherent and convincing account of the Air's discovery and development, some details remain unclear and require further research - in particular:

(i) the actual year in which Jane Ross heard the melody,

(ii) the precise place where she heard it,

The account does give us clues if not answers to these questions, however. As regards the year of the Air's discovery it indicates it came after a time of "famine and cholera". If, as seems likely, this refers to the great Irish famine of 1845-1849, that would imply a date from 1849 onwards. It should be remembered, however, that famines were by no means unusual in Ireland. The potato crop in Ulster had failed in 1835, and throughout Ireland in 1836, 1837 and 1839. 1841 had also seen many failures[42]. An earlier date is, therefore, possible. We know William Ross had carried the cholera victim to the cart in 1834, but the story of the Roman Catholic Priest assembling his flock "some time after" to pray for his recovery from "the fever" occurred when he was curate of Maghera (from 1839 to 1847)[40]. The suggestion of "famine fever" would, therefore, indicate a post-1846 date[42].

It seems unlikely, however, that the Air was discovered after 1850. This was the year when the Rev William Ross was instituted Vicar of Dungiven, and we know from a letter of the 4th December that year his sisters were then intending to go to England "for some time" to stay with a Mrs Pagett[5]. With his increased clerical responsibilities and impending marriage to Catherine Matilda Collins of Ham House Plymouth on the 18th of November 1851 their brother would probably have been less inclined to make lengthy journeys late at night to visit his sisters in Limavady.

Any date between 1847 and 1850 is, therefore, possible for the Air's discovery, but 1849 and 1850 remain the most likely, when the worst of the famine was already over in that part of Ireland.

We are told that "time flew" as Jane attempted to express on paper what she had heard the fiddler play, and that "presently" she was visited by Dr Petrie, but the date of that visit remains unknown. It is clear, however, that Petrie must have been given the Air in 1853, sometime between the publication of the first part of his "Collection" and the 25th of October, the date of the arrangement to be found in his papers[21].

The precise locality of the Air's discovery remains vague. It was "late one night" when Jane's brother heard it played in a "mountain cabin", and was "too pressed for time" to copy it down. The cabin must, therefore, have been close to a mountain road of which there are many in the Dungiven area. We do know, however, that the harper Hempson favoured the mountains "east inclining north of Dungiven", which would suggest Benbradagh mountain. This of course lay on the route the Rev Ross would have taken if "Connys Country" referred to the Draperstown area, as has been suggested. And it would most certainly have been a "long drive from Limavady".

While the exact location of the "mountain cabin" must remain a matter of conjecture, the slopes of Benbradagh do appear to be the most likely locality. The actual position of "Connys Country" is, therefore, unimportant.

Needless to say, the Main Street in Limavady finds no place in the Manning papers as the source of the melody, however "strong" the local traditions.

A final mystery, however, remains - how did the melody of "The Young Man's Dream" mutate so quickly and so successfully into "The Londonderry Air" as we now know it? How did it change from triple time to quadruple time, and acquire the higher section at the end which had been lacking in Bunting's original transcription? The opinion of Hugh Shields, the acknowledged expert in the folk music of the area, is surely conclusive here - the changes were the result of the "keyboard divagations of a middle class lady" – i.e. Jane Ross herself.

We now know the difficulties Jane had experienced in notating the melody and arranging it in the form in which she first heard it. She had copied it down "with sufficient notes to enable her to expand it more fully when she returned home", but never achieved this "to her satisfaction". Some form of adaptation was, therefore, inevitable. In the process the higher section at the end, which Bunting had failed to notate, was incorporated into the version she sent to Petrie, which he then published as a piano piece – much to her disappointment and "far short of the real thing". In spite of her misgivings, however, this is the version that was to achieve the worldwide fame.

The mystery is how this piano playing lady in a small country town who, as far as we know, had never studied abroad or composed another note of music in her life could have made such a successful rearrangement of an ancient Irish melody. As the most eminent of musicians have agreed, this is no ordinary folk tune but a superbly shaped melody, suffused with romantic sentiment. Could Jane Ross really have been responsible for such a creation? Perhaps. We simply do not know. The Rev Manning is silent on this subject. Her nephew, the Rev J. T. Trelawny-Ross, recalls "her delightful piano playing of all kinds of old Irish music, not least reels and dance music" without "a page of music on the piano". "The Londonderry Air", as we now have it, is very different. In the past I have speculated on a possible line of enquiry[43], but this remains speculation.

While the Manning papers remain the only written source we possess of the Air's discovery, they are unlikely to be the last word on the subject. Such is the fame of the Air and the enthusiasm of its devotees that no one account can ever hope to meet with universal approval. As we have seen, some experts have claimed the Air for County Cork and County Donegal. Others have suggested it belonged to Strabane (a letter in the "Northern Whig" of the 22nd August 1928) or Lancashire (a letter in the "Sunday Times" of the 2nd September 1928). Where such claims can be investigated the supposed link to "The Londonderry Air" as we know it is invariably tenuous, to say the least. To all such claimants the question must be posed: "If it was so well known in your locality why was it never copied down?" "The Young Man's Dream" remains the closest recorded version we possess prior to Petrie's publication of 1855. All other claimants lack the necessary written evidence.

It is this written evidence, traceable to the words of Jane Ross herself, that makes the Manning account so unique, and so highly credible.

Those who doubt its accuracy must answer two questions:
(1) Why would a well educated and widely read Anglican clergyman spend so much time and energy fabricating his account of the Air's discovery unless he believed it to be true?
(2) Why would his mother, Jane Ross's "beloved niece", have invented such a story when, at the time of her death, the Air had yet to achieve the fame that was to inspire the many subsequent legends?

Summary

The Manning papers provide a clear and coherent account of the origins and development of "The Londonderry Air" which may be summarised as follows:
c1760-1770: Denis Hempson composes a piece for the harp, based on "The Young Man's Dream", expressing his frustration at the changing musical fashions of the day, and the demise of his beloved instrument. He performs it in the Dungiven area where his older style is still appreciated. Here it is preserved by his hearers, but not shared with others.
c1849-1850: The Rev William Ross hears the melody and tells his sister Jane, who travels from Limavady to copy it down as best she can.
1853: Jane Ross entrusts the melody to Petrie.
1855: Petrie publishes the melody as a piano piece, much to her disappointment.
1855-1879: For the rest of her life Jane attempts unsuccessfully to recreate the melody as she first heard it, and dies unaware of the incredible fame that awaits its published version.
1882: The melody is first arranged as a vocal piece. Many other arrangements quickly follow.
1912: The words "Danny Boy" are added to the melody.
1915: It is recorded to these words and soon becomes "world famous".

Throughout this period "The Londonderry Air" has undergone significant changes from "The Young Man's Dream" as notated by Bunting, to the melody that was presented to Petrie by Jane Ross, and its transformation into "Danny Boy". We shall never know the part Jane Ross played in the final version of the melody, but her role was essential. Without her efforts it would have disappeared. In her adaptation it is now known the world over. For this we should all be profoundly grateful.

REFERENCES

1 *"Crockford's Clerical Directory" (1932)*
London

2 PETRIE, G. (1855)
"The Petrie Collection of the Ancient Music of Ireland" (Vols. 1 & 2),
Dublin : University Press.

3 BUNTING, E. (1840)
"A Collection of the Ancient Music of Ireland"
Dublin.

4 DAY, Angelique & McWILLIAMS, P. (1991)
"Parishes of County Londonderry 11 (1833-1835) - Roe Valley Central"
"Ordnance Survey Memoirs of Ireland" (Vol. 9)
Queens University, Belfast : The Institute of Irish Studies.

5 MULLAN, T. H. (1983)
"Limavady and the Roe Valley"
Limavady District Council.

6 *"City of Dublin and Hibernian Provincial Record" (1824)*
London : Pigot & Co.

7 McAFEE, W.
"Researching Derry and Londonderry Ancestors"
CD at Coleraine Library.

8 *"Slater's Directory of Ireland" (1846)*
Coleraine Library.

9 *"Griffith's Valuation of Ireland" (1858)*
Coleraine Library.

10 *"Slater's Directory of Ireland" (1870)*
Coleraine Library.

11 GRAVES, A. P. & STANFORD, C. V. (1882)
"The Songs of Old Ireland"
London.

12 GRAVES, A. P. & HINKSON, KATHERINE (1894)
"The Irish Song Book"
Dublin.

13 MANN, A. (2013)
"In Sunshine and in Shadow: The Family Story of Danny Boy"
Lulu.com

14 BRISTOL POST (2013)
www.bristolpost.co.uk/life-local-man-song-Ireland-loves/story-19452033-detail/story.html

15 COLEMAN, H. (1918)
"The Londonderry Air"
Musical Times, August 1918, p. 349-350.

16 *"Ancestry Library Edition" (2011)*
Coleraine Library

17 CRAWFORD, R. (1897)
"The Crawfords of the County Donegal"
Dublin.

18 WALFORD, E. (1919)
"Walford's County Families of the United Kingdom"
London.

19 O'SULLIVAN, D. (1958, new edition 2001)
"Carolan, The Life, Times and Music of an Irish Harper"
London (p. 272).

20 GALWEY, Honoria (1910)
"Old Irish Croonauns and Other Tunes"
London: Boosey & Co.

21 AUDLEY, B. (2002)
"The Londonderry Air : Facts and Fiction"
http://web.archive.org/web/20050930170319/http://pages.britishlibrary.net/londonderryair

22 FOX, Charlotte Milligan (1912)
Journal of the Irish Folk Song Society, (Vol. 12).

23 HUNTER, J. (1998)
"O'Hampsey – The Last of the Bards"
Centre for Irish Literature and Bibliography,
University of Ulster, Coleraine.

24 CHADWICK, S. (2009)
www.earlygaelicharp.info/rorydall/rory-dall-tune-list.pdf

25 MOULDEN, J. (editor) (1979)
"Songs of the People" (part 1)
Belfast (p. 35).

26 HUNTER, J. (1997)
"The Blind Fiddler from Myroe"
Centre for Irish Literature and Bibliography,
University of Ulster, Coleraine.

27 HUNTER, J. (2000)
"Jane Ross and the Londonderry Air"
Centre for Irish Literature and Bibliography,
University of Ulster, Coleraine.

28 PARRY, H. (1893)
"The Art of Music",
London.

29 BRIAN, H. (1935)
"On the Other Hand", by La Main Gauche,
Musical Opinion, February 1935, p. 395.

30 GILCHRIST, Anne Geddes (1934)
"A New Light upon the Londonderry Air",
Journal of the English Folk Dance and Song Society, Vol. 1, no. 3.

31 SHIELDS, H. (1979)
"New Dates for Old Songs, 1766-1803",
Long Room, nos. 18-19,
Dublin : Trinity College Library.

32 BUNTING, E. (1796)
Original manuscripts,
Queen's University, Belfast.

33 BUNTING, E. (1797)
"A General Collection of the Ancient Irish Music",
Dublin.

34 AUDLEY, B. (2000)
"The Provenance of the Londonderry Air",
Journal of the Royal Musical Association, Vol. 125, no. 2 : 205-247.

35 FITZSIMONS, E. & SMITH, J. (1814)
"Irish Minstrelsy: A Selection of Original Melodies of Erin with Characteristic Words by Edward Fitzsimons, Esq. and Symphonies and Accompaniments by Mr. J. Smith,"
Dublin.

36 DAY, Angelique & McWILLIAMS, P. (1992)
"Parishes of County Londonderry 1V (1824, 1833-1835) - Roe Valley Upper: Dungiven"
"Ordnance Survey Memoirs of Ireland" (Vol. 15)
Queens University, Belfast : The Institute of Irish Studies.

37 BUNTING, E. (1809)
"A General Collection of the Ancient Music of Ireland"
London.

38 YEATS, Grainne (1992)
"The Harp of Ireland"
Belfast : Belfast Harpers' Bicentenary Ltd.

39 FOX, Charlotte Milligan (1911)
"Annals of the Irish Harpers"
London.

40 *"Crockford's Clerical Directory"* (1885)
London.

41 MAWHINNEY, G. (1996)
"The McHenry Letters (1834-1846)"
Ballinascreen Historical Society.

42 WOODHAM-SMITH, Cecil (1962)
"The Great Hunger - Ireland 1845-1849"
London.

43 DRUMMOND, B. (2010)
"A Long Drive from Limavady",
The Journal of Music, (Vol. 2, no. 2).